FAIRYDUST TO DAFFODILS

A Memoir

Also by Patricia Steele ~
"Living with Cystic Fibrosis" in *Your Health Magazine*

Standalone Fiction:
Tangled like Music
Cloisonné

Callinda Beauvais Mystery Series:
Shoot the Moon, 1
Wine, Vines and Picasso, 2
Thorny Secrets and Pinot Noir, 3
Flamenco Strings: Uncorked, 4

Travel Memoirs:
A Roundabout Passage to Venice
Mind the Gap in Zip it Socks

Cooking DRUNK (and wine tasting 101), a cookbook
Goodbye Balloon, a children's story
A Thousand Heartprints

By Patricia Ruiz Steele
Spanish Pearls Series:
Book One: The Girl Immigrant
Book Two: Silván Leaves
Book Three in Progress: Ruiz Legacies

FAIRYDUST TO DAFFODILS
A Memoir

Patricia Steele

A memoir: A child with cystic fibrosis and her mother's choices

She was born amidst fairydust and left us when yellow daffodils
blanketed the ground

ISBN: 9780989001342
Cover image photo: SelfPubBookCovers.com/LesDale
Book cover: Christopher Howard ~ WWW.blondesign@gmail.com

Visit the author website: www.patriciabbsteele.com

IN MEMORIAM

Christina "Chrissy" Marie Dixon-Zaccone
1969-1978

~

My deep-felt thanks to my mother, Neyda Bettencourt;
Without reading the notes in her diary from 1969-1978, my
memory would have been too shadowy to write this memoir. She is my
rock. Without her daily journal to kick start some of these memories, I
could not have written this book.

A special hug to my children,
Frank J. Zaccone and Audrie (Zaccone) Abernathy
I hope this memoir makes your big sister more real to you.

And to their father, Frank Zaccone, who loved my child as his own

Acknowledgements

Names fly through my mind and I can't hold onto them, so I will begin at the beginning. Many friends and family members provided me with emotional support during the most difficult years of my life and encouraged me to complete this book. Helpful beyond measure include my parents, Neyda and Koffee, my brothers, Rick, Steven and Carl, and the Berger family with their daughters, Sister Mary and Tina.

Thank you Sophia Leslie, Sheryl Linderman, Sally Newhardt and Dr. Julia Grach. I also thank friends and family in Ohio who treated Chrissy like she belonged; Deborah and Judy Zaccone, Cynthia Kessler, Maggie Peduzzi, Chuck and Gloria Herring, Aunt Violet and Uncle Matt Zaccone, Joseph and Josephine Zaccone, Pamela Key, Nancy Donofrio Earl, Dali O'Doherty, Janie and Bernie Lane, Maxine Gates, Lavonna and Donna Redmond. These people gave of themselves and shared their deepest feelings with me during the course of time they were in my life.

Thank you, Linda Dixon Schmalz for living through your pain again by reading this story to help identify errors, my only beta reader.

When my dear friend Roberto Wilcox mentioned the fact that I'd finished Chrissy's story on Mother's Day, I smiled.

Most especially, I thank the two people in my life who will see Chrissy through my eyes in a special way and understand my obsession with finishing her story. Her siblings -- Frank Joseph Zaccone and Audrie L. Zaccone Abernathy. To you, my children, I hope the photos at the end of this memoir will bring her alive for you and you can feel her embrace.

I believe that there are no bad days if you are breathing. Cystic Fibrosis is not new; a lot of these children do not grow up into adulthood. We fought the odds and focused on the positives rather than the negatives. In short, we wanted Chrissy to live, but it was not to be. I cried gallons of tears as I tried several times during the past forty years to write this memoir.

CHAPTER ONE
PROLOGUE

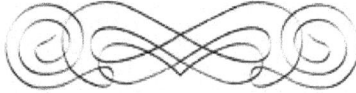

Oregon Health Science University (OHSU)
Portland, Multnomah, Oregon
February 24, 1978

The long, stark corridors echoed with silence. I thought sitting alone would ease my anxiety, my weariness, but it didn't. I'd never felt so alone in my entire life. Of course, the solitude was only in my mind; I could hear sporadic whisperings of soft conversation drift towards me as I sat in my daughter's hospital room. Antiseptic scented the room along with the odor from her IV tape and more.

The nurse's steady vigilance at the nearby medical station did, however, give me that needed measure of assurance I craved. They had all become our friends, practically family, during Chrissy's hospital stay at Doernbecker Children's Hospital, located on SW Sam Jackson Park Road at the top of a hill above the Willamette River at OHSU. They watched over Chrissy like mother ducks and monitored her breathing closely. They also watched over me and held me up when I faltered.

My eyes wandered for the hundredth time to the solitary bed in the corner of the cream-colored room. The table overflowed with get-well cards, as did the window ledge and stark wall above the narrow bed where my lovely, sleeping child lay. A vibrant, red amaryllis sat on the window sill against the backdrop of a snow-covered mountain. The nurses measured its growth daily to entertain her. On a clear day, the view of Mt. Hood took one's breath away. Tonight, it was Chrissy's breath I worried about.

Tonight, her small, sleeping face was calm and gentle. I marveled at the innocence and vulnerability I saw stamped on her soft, even features lit by the glow of a night light. Her frail body was nearly swallowed by the pillow and the surrounding bundle of bedding. Her hair lay scattered across her pillow like golden strands of sunshine, a beautiful and unfair contrast to her ashen, freckled face, which was smooth as silk. Awake, she had vivid blue, almond-shaped eyes that sat above high cheekbones and one dimpled cheek. Her eyes usually twinkled with excitement...but they were not twinkling tonight. They hadn't twinkled in a long time.

I sighed into the dark room, glad my mother sat nearby. She was my rock. Her face was etched with sadness. It certainly didn't ease the stone lodged in my belly. She slept fitfully, each of us afraid to leave.

Glancing back toward Chrissy, I smiled. She was short for her age, like I was, but she didn't seem to mind. Despite being just a touch under nine years old, a little wise-woman inhabited her body. A gifted child, sometimes set apart by her classmates, she felt loved by too many friends to count. Mostly, they protected her and frowned at those who mimicked her gut-wrenching coughs.

Chrissy has Cystic Fibrosis. The Mayo Clinic defined the children's disease as a life-threatening disorder that causes severe damage to the lungs and digestive system. It is an inherited condition and affects the cells that produce mucus, sweat and digestive juices. These secreted fluids are normally thin and slippery. But in Cystic Fibrosis, a defective gene causes the secretions to become thick and sticky. Instead of acting as a lubricant, the secretions plug up tubes, ducts and passageways, especially in the lungs and pancreas. Cystic Fibrosis is most common in white people of Northern European ancestry, but also occurs in Hispanics, African-Americans and some Native Americans. It is rare in people of Asian and Middle Eastern origin. Cystic Fibrosis requires daily care, most people with the condition are able to attend school and with treatment, many children have lived into young adulthood.

Tonight, my girl's coughing spasms have diminished. I am relieved. Doctors have been known to be wrong. Miracles do happen. I shook my head to push yesterday's conversation from my mind. Dr. Julia Grach's face had been pinched, her eyes had been wet. I refused to give up hope. Not yet. No matter what anyone tells me. I won't. But, I saw her lips move, telling me to face the heartbreaking reality. Tears brewed. In twenty two days she should be blowing out nine birthday candles. Yes, she would!

A sigh left me without permission as I squeezed my eyes shut to hold back the tears that promised to swamp me. But they broke loose anyway. Flushed, I swept them away as fear trumped the anger and frustration I'd felt bubbling up inside for nearly nine years.

Cobwebs muddied my thoughts. I cried for Chrissy, for myself, for my family, for the unfairness of seeing my child's pain and terrible discomfort. I cried for the scientists struggling to find the cure for CF, for doctors fighting to keep patients alive; but most of all I cried for Chrissy and all the places she might never see and all the things she might never learn and the emotions she might never feel.

She had been through such a rugged ordeal during this last sojourn in the hospital. Despite many hospitalizations, it never got easier for her or those of us who loved her so well. I sat back to use the quiet time to survey my sleeping little girl. Hearing her gentle snuffling relaxed me in the darkened room. The hallway's pale shaft of light somehow managed to throw its soft beams across Chrissy's velvety features and reddish-blonde hair. I maneuvered myself around in my chair, which seemed my home-away-from-home lately, to afford me a better view of her.

I shivered at the memory of Dr. Grach's empathetic face. Our earlier conversation couldn't be real, I told myself. I wanted to vent my anger, kick the wall, and blame everyone and everything. I wanted to scream at her. The Polynesian princess, now a doctor, had enfolded me in her arms, knowing I'd wanted to run away. And we both cried. Helplessness shook my soul. So quiet. So serious. So true.

"Chrissy will not be leaving the hospital this time." She held my hand in both of hers and looked into my face, her sad, brown eyes willing me to respond. "Do you understand what I'm saying?" I tried to shake away the remembrance of her sorrowful face just inches from my own.

Tonight the small hand that I clasped tightly in my own was soft, smooth and puffy from water retention. I placed my hand over her small chest and felt her heart beating faintly beneath my palm, imagining the medication streaming through her body from the despised IV tubes. Her fingers smelled faintly of medicine and other hospital scents. The small broken veins in her hand were surrounded by yellowed, bruised areas with the unmistakable red pin prick centered within each spot. There were several. She'd been in the hospital twenty days.

Jolted back to reality, I stared at the red pricks and felt each one, stabbing into my hands, my arms and my heart. My mind was dipping and dancing. The halls were quieter now. They echoed a silence that screamed across the spaces as I sat in the darkened room, filled with the sound of my daughter's labored, rasping breath. Her small hand clutched mine, a handhold to security she no longer believed in. Her long lashes brushed her cheeks toward the tiny freckles that sprinkled over her nose.

In my head, I heard her say, "Mommy, I love you. Please don't leave me." I closed my eyes and smoothed her sleeping face with my free hand---all the while the chatter box within my mind was whispering. She will never run free, go home, share our lives, grow older, love as an adult, or have a child… or any of the things my heart demanded.

The night dragged on and unconsciously I began to rock…

My mother moved in her sleep, pulled the blanket up to her chin. The day had been riddled with heart-stopping experiences and I was numb from the emotional trauma. I laid my head back on the chair, feeling the last three weeks slip through me as I tried to reason with the facts, fantasies and lost dreams. I closed my weary eyes and turned my mind to the first surreal moments of her life far away from the bittersweet sadness of today.

PART ONE

CHAPTER TWO

March 15, 1969

My face ached from smiling. Watching the quirky beam of sunshine dip through the hospital window looked like sparkling fairydust. A yellow blanket swaddled her body like a cocoon. Her small face peeked out, with eyes blue as a robin's egg. She stared at me. Blink. Blink. Blink. And she was mine. All mine.

Moments earlier, the nurse had tucked the tiny, baby girl into my arms and chuckled as I snuggled my face close to inhale her baby smell. I'd called her *Thelma Yvonne* while she coiled up cozily inside my womb. I'd been sure she was a girl. But when Lance drove that damn yellow pickup truck over those wicked railroad tracks last night, the name bounced out of my head and *Christina Marie* slipped in.

I was twenty two years old, a still-naïve bride of three years. Yes, this infant had a father. Yes, I was married to him. But she was all mine, nevertheless. And I will tell you why.

It's taken me years to begin Chrissy's story and even now, I still struggle about where to begin. Her father was the rebel of his family in the tiny agricultural town when I met him the first time. I was fifteen. He was seventeen. Who said romance couldn't be found in a pole-bean yard out in the country? I picked beans with my friends, we dumped them into bags, he weighed them and I earned money for school-clothes during that summer. He was all the things my parents steered me away from. Did I listen? No. I was fifteen. I could make my own decisions.

The ill-fated romance with Lance lasted about three months until I met Tom Swanson, the sweet love of my high school life. My heartbeat accelerated, as if I was going to the prom every time I saw him. The first time he kissed me, I was over the moon. I forgot Lance the minute I set eyes on Tom's smiling face in typing class and by graduation, Tom and I were engaged. My parents didn't like it, but we were in love. Really? We were both seventeen in 1964.

And life was divine.

Until the summer after graduation and the real world opened up...

Tom went to college in Canoga Park, California and I moved to Portland, Oregon with my family. When we both realized there was a world out there, our engagement promises slipped away. But the memories forever after, did not. I found a secretarial job at Northwest Insurance, earned $210 a month. I was rich. I drove my own car, a 1956 red and white Ford. What a great little car it was too. Dad loaned me $500 to buy it. I sat up all night looking down at my little Ford from my bedroom window with the moonlight shining off its metal like a bonfire. A car of my own.

§

Lance slipped back into my life the minute he learned Tom was gone and by the summer of 1965, I was walking down the aisle. My Dad told me if I had sex before I got married, he could tell by the way I walked the next morning. What? Lance, the rebel, wanted to challenge his words. But Dad's words were stronger than any lure. So, Lance married a naïve virgin and I realized, too late, that it was a romp in bed he wanted, not a lifetime companion.

Our marriage was rocky from the beginning. Despite the bright and shiny wedding rings on our fingers, our lives were not what either of us had imagined. We lived in a tiny logging town in the woods near the Rogue River in Oregon. He praised me for my housekeeping abilities and we brushed up on our lovemaking after the disappointing honeymoon night when neither of us completely undressed because I was so nervous. Lance thought his prowess in bed was tops. I didn't want to hurt his feelings by telling him otherwise. Oh, god, did I just say that?

For the first two months of our marriage, life was fun. He left at dawn, rode in a vehicle called a *crummy* with a load of other men and logged in the woods. I played house in our very tiny 28' x 8' trailer house that sat in the corner of a farmer's back acreage. When we added Tracy, a small fox terrier puppy, to our home – our life was almost a holiday.

Despite feeling lonely away from my family, I was learning to be an adult. I wrote letters, cleaned our trailer and baked. One day, I made maple bars. Coming from a family of six, it was difficult for me to get the hang of cooking for two. And the maple bar recipe? I'd forgotten it made dozens. In the small trailer, there weren't many flat areas to lay them out to cool. When I cooled and frosted them...it seemed like there were a hundred spread around on the counter, the stove top, the arms and back of the couch. Of course, Tracy was too small to jump up on the couch, right? Wrong. When I turned around, that little puppy was eating the maple bars as fast as her little jaws could chomp. I had a fit. I cut off all her teeth marks, moved everything to the double bed and closed the door. Her reproachful eyes made me laugh.

I enjoyed our sexual freedom those first weeks. However, sex wasn't all I wanted. I wanted a friend, a confidant. When Lance was laid off from his logging job, our life changed and the laughter started to die down. By Thanksgiving, I knew I'd made a terrible mistake as I watched him flirt with other women and tip too many beers. He promised to change, so we moved our trailer north to Albany where he worked in town, but it was so different from our life in the woods. There were more people. More bars. More women.

Our honeymoon was over.

And then, someone in the trailer park poisoned Tracy.

I washed our clothes at his parent's house weekly before finding a job as a secretary for a collection agency. I hated the job, but it helped pay the bills. Lance's propensity for flirting stayed just under the radar until one day I drove to his mother's house to do our laundry. I found a revealing note pushed into the steering wheel of our car when I prepared to drive home again. The woman evidently thought Lance was there, not his wife.

We'd been married six months.

Everything changed in the blink of an eye.

I accused.

He denied.

But I refused to give up. Life bumpily continued until he enlisted in the U.S. Army. With the distance between us, life was good. When I realized I was pregnant, I moved to Portland to live with my parents. After I miscarried our child, his Army unit sent him to Vietnam and I found a job in Portland.

Funny how being apart makes you forget all the bad times. We exchanged letters every week and a germ of hope grew. A few months later, I asked my employer to give me a week off to fly to Hawaii to meet Lance on what the military called R & R, rest and relaxation/recuperation. I nearly got fired over it. I went anyway. Lance had been in Vietnam for several months and being together again felt like a honeymoon; we almost forgot why he left. Maybe we were growing up?

When he returned from Vietnam, he suffered from the horrors he lived through over there. He'd sometimes wake up in a sweat, flailing his arms and crying. I learned quickly to be wary. I tiptoed around him when he slept because his reactions could be brutal and swift. He'd seen his friends blown up, mutilated, dying and worse.

Now, he would be stationed at Fort Ord near Monterey, California. The good news was that I loved traveling and moving to California sounded like a great adventure. The bad news was he wanted me to trade in my little 1956 Ford for an El Camino pickup. It would carry everything for the move, he argued. It broke my heart to give her up, but my disease to please was in full gear. I gave in. I later learned the car dealership sold it for $75.

Monterey, California in 1968 was beautiful. We found a sweet duplex above a garage near the beach; we could hear sea lions nearby and the sound of the surf lulled us to sleep each night. I painted the apartment walls in exchange for rent credit. The kitchen had a small nook and shelving that I painted white with yellow trim. It took me three full days to scrub the nastiness out of the ceramic-tiled shower until the entire place sparkled. I played house again and everything was as I'd hoped. The smells of the ocean seeped into the apartment and I was happy.

Lance found a turquoise 1965 Mustang, so we traded in the El Camino. Selling kids a car with no down payment and high interest made sense for the car lot. All we cared about was that the monthly car payment amount didn't increase. We didn't focus on the interest at all.

I made friends with the people around me and cried with my new neighbor when she lost her baby boy to SIDS. Gut wrenching sobs accompanied her grief as I listened to her sadness and my tears mingled with her heartache. I couldn't imagine her pain. How could one bury a child? Her vacant stare and wet eyes told me it wasn't anything I wanted to face. She'd whisper his name, hold tightly to her breasts as milk leaked through her blouse and cry some more.

Our roof landing was a perfect place to lay a blanket and lounge on the space between both duplexes. With the sounds of the surf a few blocks away and the warm sun above, I read a book until I became drowsy and fell asleep. I burned both legs so badly that my neighbor had to drive me to Fort Ord's emergency room. Pain shot through my calves like bullets; my tight, red skin throbbed and screamed.

After hobbling inside, the doctor yelled at me, "Don't you know when to come inside out of the sun? Even my *children* know that!" He tossed a tube of cream at me to rub on the burns. It bounced off my lap and onto the floor. Stunned, I stumbled out of there and swore I'd never go back. My blistered legs pulsated and kept me awake for three nights, cream and all. But, from then on, I did know when to come in out of the sun.

The joy of living in Monterey was multiplied by the proximity to the beach, sand and wonderful weather. It was an easy walk to feel sand between my toes and listen to the ocean whisper against the rocks splashing around me. It was a lazy time for me as I walked along the beach. I tried to ignore the uneasiness and aloneness that seeped into my head. I was twenty one years old. I tried to envision my future, possibly attending school. Creative writing or interior design? I could do it, I thought. Then, I'd sigh and ask myself, how? I fantasized, not an adult after all, but I thought I was doing everything right.

§

Within two months of moving to Monterey, Lance found his army buddies more interesting than I was. He began stopping for beer at bars after work. My dinners got cold, I got angry, and he got defensive. I childishly thought a baby might save our marriage. Lance thought it was a good idea. I was willing to try anything to get our life on an even keel.

In the summer of 1968, politics was in the air. Robert Kennedy was running for president. We joined the crowd at the Monterey Airport to listen to him talk and came away pumped, ready to vote for him. It was an amazing day. Then, on June 5th, he was shot during his campaign stop in Los Angeles and died within twenty-six hours. We grieved with other Americans. America had just grieved for the loss of Martin Luther King two months earlier when he was shot and killed in Memphis, Tennessee. What was the matter with America? Our minds were numb.

By the end of that summer, Lance's army buddies begged him to re-enlist. They were offered bonus money to "re-up" and Lance was thinking about it. However, the thought of returning to Vietnam scared him.

"I don't know what I want to do, but I'm done with the Army," he said one evening. His blue eyes pleaded with me for approval.

"What do you want to do?"

He didn't answer me, but indecision lingered on his face.

"So, we return to Oregon or stay in California?" I pushed.

He stared at me. He didn't like that suggestion either. But, we mulled it over and agreed that family in Oregon tipped the scale. We gave our landlord notice and I began packing.

I knew he was restless. I could see it as each day fell into the next and his release from the Army loomed. My mind was awhirl with our discontent. I couldn't seem to make the man happy. My mind was in overdrive. Was I not pretty enough? Smart enough? Wild enough? My insecurities mounted and I felt helpless.

Lance was quiet as he drove us northward as country music blared along miles and miles of California roads. We stopped in Woodland, where I was born, to visit my aunts, uncles and cousins. Their hugs felt exquisite after Lance's parched neglect. It was a welcome change to listen to their stories, feel their hugs; I couldn't stop smiling.

Just south of the Oregon border where the mountains meet the sky and Lake Shasta is so beautiful that it takes one's breath away, Lance sighed loudly. "I've been thinking," he said as he took another lung-busting drag on his Camel cigarette. He didn't look at me, just kept his eyes on the road. "And I've decided I don't want to be married anymore."

"What?!" Heat rushed over me. I pressed my hand into my chest as if I could slow down my heartbeat, but it was still hard to breathe. I stomped my foot down on the floorboard and twisted toward him. "What if I'm pregnant? You said you wanted us to have a baby and…"

"Well, if you're pregnant, you'll have your Mom and Dad."

He blew out a tunnel of cigarette smoke and blinked through its blinding haze. I was speechless and coughed harshly from the smoke. At that moment, I wanted to pull it from his lips and smack him with its fired stub. Music continued to blare; songs of sadness and despair filled the Mustang's cab. Conversation stilled. Each song seemed to tell our story as I stared at the passing trees and mountains without seeing them. By the time we reached Albany to visit his sister Linda and her husband Stan, I was numb.

Lance remained quiet, depressed. He was frightened at the aspect of job hunting in the public sector again, but his instability frightened me more. His emotions were lopsided; he turned them on with the flip of a switch and off again the next minute. The yo-yo effect was full blown, but by the end of the weekend, he had changed his mind *again*.

"I was wrong; I want to stay with you," he said with tear-filled eyes.

My mind cracked a little; it was getting harder to pretend there was any hope for us. I was afraid; he turned affection on and off, bringing me joy one day and tears the next. I imagined pulling the petals off of a daisy…He loves me. He loves me not. He loves me. He loves me not. The swinging emotions had me tiptoeing over egg shells.

But I had made a commitment and we stuck together. We found a duplex apartment in Salem and he found a job driving a logging truck. He was like a little boy when it came to trucks and logging was all he knew since his father had logged all his life.

And yes, I was pregnant, so nobody would hire me for a job. He seemed happy about the baby, but he soon lost his job, looked for another, worked there and then got laid off. His unemployment checks barely paid the bills, but cigarettes stayed on the grocery list, absolutely. He worked hard for those smokes, he argued. In 1968, cigarettes cost $7.00 a carton and I twisted every which way but crooked to make it happen. My disease to please stayed dialed to the max.

CHAPTER THREE

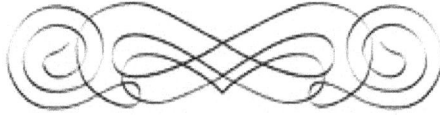

Our apartment was cozy and I made friends with neighbors on both sides of us. I became very good friends with neighbor Sally; she and her husband had a little boy and a new baby. Her house was lived in and welcoming and they had little money. She was my confidant and mentored me in my pregnancy. She made me laugh. One of my strongest memories is when she offered me lunch. She had one pork chop left from their dinner the previous night. She pulled the meat off of that single pork chop. She spread it across two sandwiches, added an onion slice, a bit of mayonnaise and a tiny leaf of lettuce. Delicious. I enjoyed it more than I relish a steak today.

On the other side of us, lived an older woman, neighbor Shelley, her husband and little boy. It was hard to connect with her. She was distant; slim, tan, and pretty. Her home was spotless and I envied her fancy decor. Her dyed black hair, always perfection, set off startling blue eyes. She would wave to me as she watered her potted flowers, wearing skimpy sundresses and strappy sandals. Her little boy was a terror.

She, however, surprised me one day by inviting me to a movie. Starved for an outing, I agreed. I didn't like the movie or her questions as her eyes darted between me and the road when she drove us home.

"Does Lance tell you he loves you very often? Do you spend time together in the evenings? You know, watching TV or just talking? Jack and I are having a few problems and I just wondered how often other men told their wives how they felt....?"

I wasn't sure how to answer and thought she was rude to ask such a question. "Well….he tells me more with actions than words." I had no intention of answering the questions she peppered me with all the way home. Something just didn't feel right, but I ignored the voices in my head.

Shelley, worldly and confident, continued to bother me as my pregnant belly ballooned. I was jealous of her trim figure, decorating skills, summer tan, and the easy way she had with men. She could have stepped off the cover of Vogue. Sometimes I'd watch her from my kitchen window while she pulled weeds and planted flowers dressed in a little sundress. Who gardens in a sundress?? Her little strappy sandals and polished toe nails made me smile; her clothes always matched her shoes. To this day, I never leave the house unless everything matches, my make-up on, hair combed, everything in place. Funny how one person, who gives you such grief, can cross your life's path and make such a lasting impression? But I digress.

When I first noticed Lance's attraction to her, I refused to believe it. Yes, I was naïve. It started with the little things and it pushed my self-esteem into crunch mode as it sped downhill fast.

Lance and Jack were becoming good friends and he was spending a lot of time at their apartment, which was only steps away from our kitchen's sliding-glass doors. In fact, he soon spent more time there than at home. I tried not to imagine them together, telling myself Lance was there for Jack.

But through those troubling months, I loved being pregnant. When the first butterfly-feeling blipped in my belly, I froze with the thrill of it. I tried to imagine the tiny being growing inside of me and then holding her in my arms.

My family in Portland was cautiously happy.

I started crocheting blankets and booties while my mother and godmother Ellen Berger began buying tiny clothes, blankets, diapers. Our baby's room soon looked like a nursery. My mother-in-law was overjoyed and began making us little blankets too. My sister-in-law couldn't stop grinning at the thought of becoming an auntie to my child. It was bittersweet because Linda had delivered a baby boy a few years earlier. He'd been born with Cystic Fibrosis and her baby had died days after his specialized surgery.

Cystic Fibrosis ran rampant through their family; my youngest brother-in-law suffered with the disease and two of their siblings had died at early ages, both gone before they entered school. I was told the disease required both parents to be carriers of the recessive gene that caused CF.

In those days, the internet was a whisper in the future; I wrote a letter to John Hopkins Medical Center. Their Cystic Fibrosis Clinical Researcher responded. "Do not worry; if this disease has never surfaced in your family history, your child should be healthy." So, I set aside my worries and concentrated on my growing baby. My OB/GYN, Dr. Wood, assured me everything was normal.

My Mom gave us a little chest of drawers that soon held diapers, tiny t-shirts, plastic pants, lotions and receiving blankets. Some days I fondled each piece, ran my hands over their softness and visualized my baby in the miniature crib that had previously belonged to my little brother Carl. I rolled it around to fit in the corner, moved it along the wall, put blankets in, pulled them out, stacked diapers. I counted the days toward March.

In Oregon, the logging industry is seasonal. Snow covered the forested hills in the winter. By thanksgiving, Lance had been laid off for more than a month and we couldn't pay our rent.

Lance suggested I call the landlord. "Tell him we're broke, you're pregnant and we can't even pay the electricity bill to keep the heat on because I'm not working."

"Please Lance, you need to call."

He pleaded with me for three days before I relented. I felt like crap but he assured me that a pregnant woman during winter without heat would get farther than he would. So, I made the call. The landlord was very nice; he gave us one month to catch up. I glared at Lance and he thrust a fist to the air with a smug grin on his face.

A couple weeks later, Lance and neighbor Jack decided they needed time away from their women, a little visit to the bar, a few beers. He kept some money from his unemployment checks. Neither neighbor Shelley nor I liked the idea. I hated to spend a penny on beer when we couldn't pay our rent and I said so.

"Your pregnancy has turned you into a nag," Lance muttered.

Still out of work, he was depressed and moody. I thought maybe a night out would perk him up. Maybe I *was* becoming a nag. He showered, shaved, put on cologne and left with a smile on his face. I felt guilty for enjoying the solitude and peace he left behind.

During those weeks, neighbor Sally and I spent a lot of time together with her little boy and her baby. She got me hooked on soap operas as my belly grew. I smiled more. Some days, she'd tap my baby bump and lean close, "Hello in there."

Life in our household went from bad to worse.

Lance started having lengthy phone conversations with Jack every evening on our bedroom phone. "I'm going to call Jack" became a nightly litany. One night, I heard part of Lance's sentence as I came down the hallway and there was no doubt in my mind that it was neighbor Shelley he was talking to, not her husband Jack.

"Lance, that's not Jack, is it? It's Shelley." My heart rate sped up and I white knuckled the door frame.

He whispered into the phone and hung up, challenging me with his eyes. "What are you accusing me of?"

I stared at him.

"If you're accusing me of something, then maybe I should do it." Blue eyes that once smiled warmly now held an aggrieved glare.

Just before Christmas, I ran away despite being six months pregnant. When I walked into my parent's house with a packed bag and a face crumpling with tears, they welcomed me. By this time, they surely had skid marks on their tongues holding back their anger at their son-in-law.

After a week, Lance called from the neighbor's. We'd lost our own phone service because he'd been laid off. "I need my wife back."

Really? I couldn't answer him.

"I want to come see you on Sunday."

Against my better judgment, I agreed. I knew my parents were annoyed because they were spitting mad at him, but he was a sweet talker. When Lance arrived, he wasn't alone. Jack and Shelley were with him and they had already stopped for dinner. Did I want some leftovers? Lance asked me when I was coming home. I crossed my arms over my big belly and turned on my heel. I'm sure my glare would have fried eggs on the sidewalk.

My parents were supportive. Although they thought eighteen was too young to get married, I had assured them I knew my own mind. Now, three years later with a pregnant daughter back home, they tried to balance their misgivings, but I knew they wanted to slap Lance silly.

Dad had always encouraged him to get a trade, but Lance loved driving big trucks with chrome wheels. Dad still tried to stay neutral, but I could see his patience wearing thin.

Lance arrived again a few days later, crying those baby blues, practically down on his knees. "I paid the phone bill and you can call your Mom any time you want to, okay?"

Yes, I gave in.

Mom and Dad masked their disappointment, gave us their best wishes again and I saw hope flit across their faces. Maybe this time…

When we returned to Salem, I learned that neighbor Shelley had cooked our frozen turkey, I burst into tears. I was angry because she baked it without stuffing. I loved stuffing. Lance tried to be patient with my mood swings. He was called back to work again. I was thrilled…we could afford to buy groceries again. We'd been eating the free food my father-in-law brought us from the food bank; cheese, dried eggs, crackers and peanut butter. And we were happy to have it.

I kept a pregnancy journal and listed all the times my baby was awake all through February. Who knows why? I laugh as I look at my journal pages and wonder what all the stars are scribbled beside the morning and evening times jotted on each page. Hiccups? Feeling that little person rolling and rooting around inside me was the most amazing thing that had ever happened to me in my life.

By late February, the private phone calls started again. I denied their affair in order to retain my pride. Lance had taken the words, love thy neighbor literally; I would see Shelley drive away in her fancy car and then I'd count to ten before Lance said he had an errand to run and he was gone.

Neighbor Shelley and I pretended life was normal. But inside my naïve persona lurked a Nancy-Drew mentality. It wasn't really a mystery by then, but I made it so. I'd become adept at avoiding reality during my life, so if I didn't confront the liaison, it wasn't happening.

During my growing up years, I had learned to keep my mouth shut. I wasn't allowed to argue or say anything that would hurt others. In other words, be a good girl and step back. Others are in control. Unfortunately, those rules taught me that standing up for myself was unacceptable. Telling others when something wasn't right, was unacceptable. Sometimes a little lie here and there was more acceptable than facing the consequences of an angry and sometimes cantankerous father.

I realized, during those last weeks of my pregnancy, that I had traded a Dad who drank a bit too much and had a short fuse for a husband who did the same. But Dad took his commitments to heart, unlike Lance who could ignore it like water rolling down the drain.

As my pregnancy progressed, I told myself I was transferring my anger from Lance to Shelley. When my OB/GYN asked me why I appeared so sad at my appointment, I burst into tears and the story came out in jerky sentences. He handed me a Kleenex and pulled up a chair.

"Do you think your husband is having an affair with this woman?" His eyes stared into mine. "Or do you think you are feeling big, unattractive and just a bit jealous of her right now?"

"I don't know! They are together a lot and he follows her when she drives away from the house. When he walks over to their apartment, I think maybe he's not there long enough to…."

Dr. Wood rolled his thumb across his lips. "Well, you know it doesn't take very long to have sex when you want it."

My head jerked upward in shock. He reached for my hand. "Give it time. Have your baby. Maybe it's not happening at all. I'm just saying, don't ignore it. Instead, talk to your husband. Get it out in the open because it won't disappear by pretending it away and you don't need the stress right now. If it is true, you'll know what you must do for this little one." He patted my belly and gave me a smile.

By March 1st, Lance was laid off again. When Mom and Ellen arrived to visit me, Lance's depression was reflected in his grumpiness when he ordered me around. I was too tired and felt too bulky to argue with him. I brought him whatever he asked for and tried to ignore the disgusted looks on the women's faces. His churlishness wasn't new and I was too tired to get angry. All I could think about was Dr. Wood's words.

.

That evening after Mom left, Johnny Cash's country voice filled the apartment. The record player was in the bedroom, so Lance had the volume very loud so he could hear it in the rest of the house. I felt a headache begin to erupt behind my eyes. I turned down the radio's volume, drew the words in my head and walked toward the kitchen. I was eager to talk to him with the doctor's words fresh on my mind. I found Lance standing in front of the glass sliding doors. It was dusk. I could see him making hand signals across the way. And then I saw Shelley was there…responding with a grin on her face. When she saw me, she jumped back inside her doorway. Lance turned around slowly to stare at me as he raised his hands to close the blinds.

That's when I began thinking of this baby as mine, mine alone.

My heart knew I'd be raising this child without a father, but dammit I did not want to fail at my marriage. The doctor's promised due date was March 3rd and I counted the days every morning by drawing a big X on the calendar days. I was feeling fat, grumpy and ready. I only weighed 136 pounds, proof that we were not eating right.

Just a little longer, I vowed.

CHAPTER FOUR

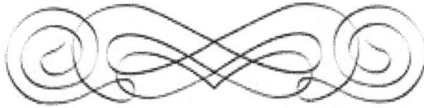

Something tickled my subconscious. I fought against the intrusion and pushed away with my hand as if a pesky fly buzzed me. I was hot and then cold, tossing off the covers and then yanking them back again.

"Babe, wake up! Is it time?"

Trying to sit up in the bed while still groggy, I pushed both hands through my hair and opened one eye. "What?" Lance was half crouched beside me. I was surprised at the worried frown etched across his forehead.

He straightened up to his medium tall height. His short-sleeved, blue shirttail hung outside his Levis, wrinkled and disheveled. He reeked of beer and cigarettes. "I heard you moaning all the way from the living room. I guess I fell asleep on the couch because the television is still on. Are you in labor?" His shaking hands pulled away the bedspread.

We looked at one another. "Do you think it's real this time?" I'd spent the previous weekend in Salem Memorial Hospital with false labor and the disappointment afterward made me afraid to hope. When a contraction speared the small of my back, I clutched the sheet and held my breath. I kept hearing Dr. Wood's words, "Don't worry, Patricia. You'll know when labor begins…you'll just know." And I knew this was it.

I looked at Lance and pointed toward his watch. We timed the contractions at six minutes apart, for once sharing the excitement. "Put my bag into the car and I'll get ready." My voice sounded hoarse.

Lance nodded his head. I saw something in his blue eyes I hadn't seen for a while. He placed his hands on my shoulders to help me stand up, as if, suddenly, I was precious to him. Without a word, he grabbed my bag and rushed down the hallway.

After I pushed my legs into the stretch pants I'd worn for so many months and jerked the burgundy smock over my head, I stood still and cocked my ear. Disbelief washed over me. Was he revving up that yellow bomb of a pickup for our trip to the hospital instead of the car? I squeezed my brown eyes closed, smoothed a shaking hand over my bulging belly and wanted to scream. Would I ever understand this man who was my husband?

I wanted to spit. Instead, I gritted my teeth and grappled with my pink wool coat trying to button it over my belly with shaking fingers. With my purse clutched tightly beneath my arm, I walked doggedly toward the front door.

Lance hurried toward me, limping slightly. His hip must be hurting him again, I thought distractedly, but he was acting like the old Lance who was thoughtful, charming and loving. His eyes sparkled. I grimaced, thinking about how cloudy and smoky they looked when he was angry. I tried to ignore the rattling noise coming from the driveway. Instead, I thought of the baby I would surely embrace in the next few hours.

Lance guided my ungainly body up onto the running board and into its shaking cab. His calloused fingers gripped my wrist and elbow as he helped me into the seat. His puzzled look surprised me, as if he was weighing his next words. Then, he shrugged, ran to the driver's door and jumped behind the wheel. When he glanced at me, I saw indecision, a little guilt. Was he wondering what happened to us? Was he thinking about being a beast the past few months? Was he thinking about how the freckles on my face were splattered across my nose? Was he thinking about his restlessness, his inability to commit to anything or anyone? Was he thinking how nice it would be when I wasn't fat anymore? My mind was flipping around like a kaleidoscope.

"You doin' okay?" He stared at me.

Shaking, I concentrated on what was happening inside my body. There was a brand new life to think about. Why was I wasting precious time feeling sorry for him? Analyzing him? I caressed my belly and shook my head to focus. Could my baby's birth possibly dissolve so many months of unhappiness? No. And then I couldn't stop the words from falling from my mouth. "Why are we driving the pickup?"

He looked at me and frowned as he shoved the gear shift and threw it into reverse. "You know I don't like being seen in that old Ford." He spit out the word Ford as if it was dirt.

"That *old* Ford is only eight years old and much more comfortable than this jazzed-up truck that shakes the bejesus out of us. What are you thinking?" I squeezed my eyes shut as the tires jumped over the edge of the cement driveway into the street. Every bump reverberated through my quaking body and with each jolt my resentment grew. Who on earth would see him driving my car at two in the morning and who the hell cared?

The streets were dark as we passed through the city. I moved in tandem with the jerks, motions and bumps, but my feet could barely reach the floorboard. I tried to cushion the vibrations shooting through my back by pressing my toes against the floor, but when he jolted across the first set of railroad tracks, another contraction smashed into me. When I arched upward off the seat, a bizarre sense of unreality screamed words inside my head. I vowed, when this baby is born, she would be all mine.

Suddenly, as the crusty truck rolled over another set of uneven steel rails, my mind cooled to a standstill. Country music blared around us. I glanced toward Lance against the blackness of the windows. The lighted dashboard illuminated the contours of his face while his burning cigarette flared against the darkness.

My body didn't feel like it was my own. Fingers of calmness caressed my mind like a breath of fresh air and happiness mixed with nonsense. I was sometimes impulsive and often oversensitive. It was unusual for me to be nonsensical, but a sense of wonder crept over me. With each labored breath, I knew I wasn't dreaming. It was definitely real; I would deliver a baby girl and her name would be Christina Marie, not Thelma Yvonne, after all. As Christina's name floated into my mind like a whispery kiss, the epiphany made me smile.

Lance must have seen the conflicting emotions cross my face when his truck bounced over the last set of tracks. I saw him wince. He slowed down and looked at me, lifted an eyebrow.

"It's a girl, Lance." I whispered.

"Oh no. I made a boy, I told you that." He reached out one work-worn hand to pat my protruding belly as he steered with the other.

I smirked. Something beautiful was happening and words tumbled through my mind the remainder of the trip to the hospital. I wanted love, but I knew that the love I needed was not going to come from him. I needed stability, trust and a strong commitment. I needed a man to give, as well as to accept responsibilities that go hand in hand with marriage. I was waking up to real life and a great weight lifted away.

I shook my head sadly as I glanced at Lance that dark night, believing that he felt obligated to be with me. One day he'd said, "You shouldn't have to work at a marriage. It's either good or it isn't." My future with him had wavered that day and inched out that window for me. I now saw a blank slate. I closed my eyes and rested my head back on the brown vinyl upholstery and groaned. If only the truck's incorrigible shaking would stop.

Lance turned down the radio and patted my knee. "Almost there."

I ignored him and didn't open my eyes. I envisioned an infant that I could nurture and cherish in a way he had denied me. The new life would give meaning in place of the chaos. And I would be important to my child as she would be to me.

As the lights loomed before us, the brain-rattling pickup reached the emergency entrance to Salem Memorial Hospital. I strained against the body blow when Lance slammed his foot on the brake. Throwing me off balance as he ground the gearshift into park, he jumped out to grab a wheelchair from the hospital's emergency room lobby.

I rolled my eyes as he ran around to help me down. He grabbed my bag and eased me into the wheelchair as a nurse met us with a sheaf of questions. Her bright red hair was frizzed beyond the framework of her pinched, dark face. She grimaced in what some might mistake for a smile and gripped the handles of the wheelchair.

Lance followed us with my bag.

While I was being prepared for delivery, he paced up and down the dimly-lit hallway and puffed on cigarettes. In those days, smoking was allowed everywhere. When he was finally allowed into the labor room with me, he reached for my hand. "I've fouled us up, haven't I?"

I didn't respond, but sighed deeply. He left me to pace the hallway, smoking, smoking and smoking some more. I remember thinking how strange it was for smoking to be allowed in the corridors, as the stifling smoke took one's breath away whether they wanted to inhale it or not.

By 5:00 a.m., he couldn't keep his eyes open, so the nurses pointed him to coffee. Once the sun rose, he said, "I'm going home to take a nap, babe. The nurse said it will be awhile before the baby comes and she promised to call me when you're ready to go in, okay?"

I felt a little afraid, but waved him out, ignoring the screams inside my head again. But once he was gone, the room was more peaceful, even with the broken thoughts running rampant in my head between contractions.

My friend Sally had prepared me for the labor room and then the delivery room, sharing her own experiences. She said most of the childbirth pain would be later --- in delivery, so I knew I should get a grip on myself now. I'd read magazines and books about the birthing process, but living through it was quite different. Sally had coached me in breathing and relaxation techniques and the nurses were impressed. When Sally had her first baby, a nurse had told her, "Stop fidgeting. Having a baby is like falling off a log." Sally never forgot the insensitive nurse and taught herself relaxation methods before her second child was born. And my friend shared everything she learned with me.

"Sally was right. This is definitely not like falling off a log..." Since she'd said the pain in the delivery room was worse than the labor room, I tried to get through the here and now. I inhaled and exhaled loudly between pursed lips, but I wanted to push.

Sweat poured off my face as a nurse propelled the gurney toward the delivery room at ten thirty. I was surprised to see Lance outside the door. His face was pale when he squeezed my arm. His gold, stubby beard jutted from his chin. I squeezed his calloused fingers, temporarily forgetting his betrayal.

I was drenched, tired, but pumped with excitement. I knew my baby was coming; I could feel the sharp pressure as they wheeled me into the cold, gray room. I could hear voices, "Don't push yet, honey." "Wait." "That's right." "Breathe like your friend taught you." "Just a little bit longer......" Every time I gasped for breath, they repeated their instructions but I wanted to scream at them, "I want to push now!"

When I was lifted onto a white covered bed, my legs were elevated high into two cold, steel stirrups. I was covered with a sheet and felt straps pulled across my chest. The lights shone brightly to nearly blind me. I could see women, all dressed in green, milling around the bed. Another nurse appeared, held my hand and wiped my brow. My gasps grew louder and my mind could no longer control my body. Another spasm. I tried not to whimper.

"Don't push yet, honey."

I stared at the nurse in silent misery between contractions. Squeezing my eyes tight, I could not fight off the blackness that filled my mind as each pain tore through me. The nurse continued to whisper soothingly. I waited for the pain to subside, but they seemed to be pounding at me one on top of the other. I groaned loudly, started to whimper.

"Give her the mask," said someone in white. "Offer her a whiff when the pain gets too harsh, but use as little as possible."

The mask was over my nose and mouth. The nurse's voice was muffled. I stared at the nurses above me and my eyes drooped as their faces danced in front of me. And then I couldn't keep my eyes open.

Dr. Wood's shaggy, white head came into view and he touched my hand. "You're being very brave." He smiled encouragingly. "I want you to push *only* when I tell you or you'll hurt your baby's head. It looks like you're going to stay with us this time; no Braxton Hicks contractions like last week, Patricia." He pulled his blue plastic gloves tight and his soothing voice continued to murmur encouragement.

I had faith in Dr. Wood, so I closed my eyes again until another small shriek slipped out.

"Okay, Patricia, just a minute....okay...NOW PUSH." I pushed. Hard. And squeezed the nurse's hand until it turned blue. The nurse kept wiping my forehead, smiling and nodding. I shook my head to shake off the mask, happy to feel it fall away. The doctor was massaging my belly and Christina Marie burst forth in a gentle swoosh.

"A girl!" All five pounds and thirteen ounces of her slippery body glided into my world. The feeling was exquisite and I laughed in celebration because although I was still groggy, I knew my life would never be the same; my old life was over and my new one could now begin.

"I knew it. Mom will be so happy," I cried and laughed at once.

"Your Mom?" Dr. Wood grinned. "What about your husband?" He raised his bushy white eyebrows as he began sewing me up.

"Mom wanted me to have a girl. And I wanted a girl. Lance said it was a boy, but I knew it was a girl," I babbled on.

Dr. Wood laid my baby daughter on my belly for a moment before she was lifted away to be measured and weighed. I was weary and dropped my head. Dr. Wood murmured that my baby was perfect and I'd been such a good girl. I laughed as he pulled off his gloves, patted my shoulder and left the delivery room.

The nurse was humming. "She's beautiful and perfect," she said.

I lay my tired head back down and closed my eyes. "Oh, I am so glad she's perfect. I was so worried about Cystic Fibrosis."

The nurse's head jerked upward from the medical report she was scribbling on. Several papers slid to the floor and she pursed her lips thoughtfully.

"Cystic Fibrosis?"

"Yes, of course."

"What makes you mention that, Patricia?"

CHAPTER FIVE

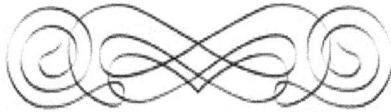

O ur eyes met in confusion.

"There's nothing in my file mentioning Cystic Fibrosis? It must be in there somewhere." My fingers pointed to her paperwork and I gripped the sheet. White noise filled my head.

She hurried over and leaned her face down to listen to me.

"Dr. Wood knows about the history in my husband's family. It's a huge medical problem and I've worried myself sick about it for a long time."

The last dregs of anesthesia drifted away as she quizzed me and saw me focus on my baby across the room. Her clear, gray eyes pondered my responses and jotted down everything I told her. It was a repetition of my fears to Dr. Wood. I had a crook in my neck because I was unable to tear my eyes away from Christina's little white rump and flailing arms, but I began my story again.

"My husband's family has been bombarded with the disease. They lost three children already. Their teenage son is still living, but he is very sick with the hereditary disease…." I rambled on.

The nurse's eyes widened with compassion as she nodded for me to continue. She stood very still with the pen poised in her hand. The room was cold, but I hardly noticed as I repeated the health history I had shared with the doctor months earlier.

Anxious to feel my baby close again, I turned toward her one last time before continuing, "I wrote to the CF Clinic in Baltimore. I received a detailed letter explaining the disease. It said both parents must carry a recessive gene in order to give birth to a CF child. Since no one in my family has been diagnosed with CF, we were told that our baby would be fine…."

I stopped talking mid-stream when Christina was bundled and placed near me for my hungry inspection. She seemed to have the gentleness of a doe as I stared at the little wonder. My joy was indescribable when I touched her soft cheek, feeling its fine gentleness under my shaking fingertips. I marveled at her perfection and was astounded at the emotions invading my body. How could such a connection be so instant and strong? All I could absorb were her huge, blue eyes in a perfectly-shaped face. Cocooned in a pale blanket, she just stared into my eyes and blinked. Stared and blinked. An intense protectiveness washed over me. While I drank in the vision of my little girl, I felt a tightness move up into my throat.

I whispered, "Oh, you *are* a Christina and you *are* perfect." We were both twenty-two; me in years, her in about as many minutes.

COMFORT. Slowly, I pulled my daughter close to my breast. "A daughter," I said aloud. Music to my ears, I said it again. "My daughter. You've made me whole." The words ran through my mind as I stared breathlessly into her face and her baby smell filled my nostrils, drowning every hospital scent around me. I began to shiver with the stunning emotions that I could never have imagined.

"Okay, little one, we must get your Mommy moved into the recovery room and show you off to your Daddy," the nurse quipped as she pulled Christina from my arms. "Your mother's shivering, see?" the smiling nurse whispered to the baby as if she understood every word.

I wasn't shivering from cold. I had never felt warmer in my life.

§

Lance had been pacing up and down the corridor since they'd wheeled me into the delivery room. Worry etched his face. His Levis clung to his hips as he frantically smoked one cigarette after another. "I know women go through this all the time, but..." he whispered to another expectant father nearby. He glanced between his watch and the big clock on the wall and squeezed the cigarette between his lips, willing the time to speed up. "Come on......" he muttered. When he turned around, puffing for a last inhalation, the nurse walked toward him.

"You have a beautiful daughter. Your wife is doing fine and she will be in her own room real soon." Her eyes drifted toward his cigarette. When he stubbed it out in the ashtray, she handed the baby to him.

Lance held the baby stiffly, afraid to move for fear of shaking something. He looked down at the nurse again, his wide-blue eyes snapping in alarm. "What do I do? How should I hold her?"

The nurse chuckled, helped him rearrange Christina in his arms and led him to a lounge chair. "Get acquainted for a moment and then she goes into the nursery." She stood beside him a moment before nodding to another nurse to take over so she could return to the delivery room.

"He's holding her and he's all smiles," the nurse told me when she returned to my side. My dreams were scattered. An optimistic hope overtook logic for the hundredth time, but only lasted for a hot minute. But, I still wanted to see his face, feel his heart and look into his eyes.

Lance reluctantly returned his new daughter to a nurse so he could follow us to my room. Once I was tucked into my bed, the nurse discreetly left us. My husband's face was wreathed in smiles. He hugged me and gently whispered, "Thank you, babe." His voice throbbed with the long-ago warmth I remembered but I knew I couldn't trust it.

He whispered, "She's beautiful." I could see he was anxious to go.

"You aren't disappointed she's a girl?" He smiled, but the moment was lost when he reached for a cigarette and said, "I better go now. You need to rest. I want to tell everyone about her. I'll call our parents and... our friends. I'll be back later, ok?"

I nodded. I knew he would tell Shelley first. Always first.

When he left, it saddened me, but I didn't dwell on it. I enjoyed being alone, being myself, without pretending I was cracking up inside. Nothing could mar the joy in my heart that day. I lay back on my pillow and stared at the ceiling. Everything smelled fresh and clean, just like my new life would be, I promised myself.

I'd grown tired of the pretense. I couldn't keep the struggle from showing or keep my mind off the situation no matter how hard I tried. How could it have gone so wrong? I blamed the rambling thoughts on the ether; nonsense drifted and rambled around in my head. Unable to stop them, I just let them rush in. Maybe Lance didn't have the capacity to share love or feel deep joy. When he was in the mood, he was everything I wanted him to be. When he wasn't, he was everything I abhorred. Maybe I expected too much from him. Maybe we just married too young…maybe, maybe, maybe. Lance was just not the man I wanted or needed anymore.

From the moment Dr. Wood confirmed my pregnancy seven months earlier, I knew she was a girl. Lance and our families laughed at my certainty and teased me whenever the subject came up in conversations. Lance's ego had refused to admit the possibility. "It's a boy and that's that," he would say with conviction to everyone who would listen. I smiled and it drove Lance to distraction. "We'll see," I'd say.

The name Thelma Yvonne, to my mother's dismay, was on my mind from the beginning of my pregnancy. Lance said the child was a boy, so he didn't care what name I chose. As a child, I was a voracious reader and my Aunt Audrie suggested I read a book titled, *Thelma,* written by Marie Corelli in 1887. The love story was about a princess from the idyllic fjords of Scandinavia married to an English aristocrat. Her name had always struck a romantic chord in my heart.

I tried to imagine my family's faces after I introduced them to Christina and then my mind stumbled and sped to Shelley. Little did I know the woman would play such a vital part in our lives within the next twenty-four hours.

CHAPTER SIX

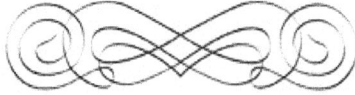

In 1969, newborn babies were housed in the Nursery, not in the new mother's room twenty four hours a day. When the baby needed nourishment, they were taken to the mother's room. Since I planned to nurse her, it wasn't long before I began fidgeting. Where was she?

When the nurse finally brought Christina to me that first time, she handed her small body to me, told me she was hungry and was gone in a flash. Holding her to my chest, I stared into her large blue eyes. She was swaddled inside a blanket. Neither of us moved for several minutes. Instead, we stared at each other, mother and daughter, each exploring the other until it dawned on me that I didn't have a clue what to do.

The deep-rooted instinct of mother love for my first-born child mesmerized me. As we stared at one another, I whispered the words aloud, "My miracle. A girl. My child. Just you and me now, kiddo." But of course, it had been just the two of us for months. I inhaled her baby smell. It was like nothing I had ever felt before and I felt sappy with emotion.

Three things filled my head. First, I vowed that no one would take my baby from me. Secondly, selfishly, I felt she was mine alone and thirdly, I refused to give Lance any more of my tears. But, I was young and vulnerable; the promises I made that day were not set in stone.

I laid Christina on the bed beside me and unwrapped her like a piece of candy. I counted her fingers and toes. They were all accounted for and I chuckled. Her arms jerked towards me like a little bird. I wrapped her warmly again, brought her to my shoulder and felt her face nuzzle into my neck.

"Oh, you sweet thing." I gently rocked her and marveled at how much this tiny being had shaken me. I remember that we stared at each other. I sang and talked to her in silly sentences until I remembered the nurse's parting words. Feed her? She wasn't crying for milk. She wasn't crying at all. What to do? I started laughing at my utter unpreparedness. I'd seen mothers nurse their babies, but never imagined actually placing my nipple into her tiny mouth without help, so I loved her with my eyes until the nurse returned.

"Uh-oh. Do you need some help?"

I shook my head and rolled my eyes in answer.

"Of course you do. This is your first child. Stupid of me."

Before I could answer, she directed Christina's mouth to my nipple. She laughed at the look on my face, gave me some instructions and fled once again.

I was afraid to move. Ever so gently, I felt the first mild tug as Christina's little mouth pulled at my breast. I closed my eyes and so did she. Contentment. I knew, after reading Sally's magazines that she was not drinking real milk because it took about three days for my milk to flow. I struggled to remember the article as the feelings created by this tiny girl hit me and I just rejoiced in the moment.

Oh. My. God. I imagined Tinkerbell's fairydust falling from the ceiling, circling and swirling around me until it filled every corner of the room, her blanket and the floor. Sparkles settled and my hands shook with mother love.

My maternal grandmother, Ella Myrtle (Chubb) Hubbard Terry had written about her own firstborn child, my Aunt Audrie and it had always stayed with me. I flipped through her poems and found the one I was looking for, "To Audrie, my First Born," that she wrote fifty-nine years earlier.

To Audrie, my First Born.

My dear little daughter
With big eyes so blue,
In my heart mother love
First woke for you.

And the day your wee body
First lay at my breast,
And I cuddled you warmly
And nursed you to rest,

My heart filled with gladness
That held no alloy,
For motherhood's glory
Was mine to enjoy

And though there are others
Now calling me mother,
Your place in my heart
Could be filled by no other.

And on your life's journey
May sorrows be few,
And Life's choicest blessings
Be showered on you.

By Ella Myrtle Terry

(My Aunt Audrie Grace Hubbard was born January 1910)

Time moved like molasses later as I waited for the room to get clogged with family and friends to see Christina. My mother beamed as she gave me gaily-wrapped packages and candy. The tiny dress for Christina was the size of a doll. Dad grinned. My friend Tina with her parents and my three brothers, Rick, Steven and Carl clamored into the room. It felt like a holiday.

I heard Lance's voice before he walked into the room alongside Shelley and her husband. How could he? I remembered curbing my anger because they looked excited to meet my new little girl, but I also remembered thinking, nastily, that I did not want her there.

Before I could tell them her name, Lance's parents, brothers and his sister Linda, who was my best friend, arrived.

It was then, with the room crowded with family that I felt like a princess because everyone waited for me to speak. "I know you're wondering why all the secrecy, but I changed her name," I said with a grin.

"Not Thelma?"

"Nope. I changed my mind. Her name is Christina Marie."

Mom made an exaggerated sigh of relief. Everyone laughed. Tina Berger was stunned as it was so close to her name, Christine. The remarks flew around the room like an uncaged bird. "She looks like a tiny bird...no, a little monkey...she's so tiny..."

Mom must have noticed that I was flagging. She shooed everyone out of the room and suddenly, I knew what my birth day must have felt like for her. She had a way of putting things right and she did it that evening.

Lance had been attentive, but it didn't sway me to change my plan. My mind was in overdrive as I imagined how long before I could take Christina to Portland and begin my life as a single parent.

When the room was empty again, I reveled in the quiet as Christina and I stared at one another again. The fairydust hadn't abated and I didn't want to relinquish her to the Nursery yet. But then my arms were empty again, the lights went off and I drifted off to sleep. And my world shifted.

It would be the last carefree moment in our lives.

Just after I nodded off that evening, our pediatrician Dr. David Sessions knocked on my door and walked in with a grave look on his face. He pulled a chair close to my bed. "Normally, I just check the newborns and make a report, but I need to talk to you a moment. Christina's initial physical exam was very good. But, there was an obstruction when I tried to insert a rectal thermometer for a temperature. It might not be serious, but I wanted to discuss it with you," he said kindly.

"What's wrong?" I fought panic from creeping over me as my words stumbled out of me. I squeezed the sheet in both fists.

He shook his head. "I'll be back in the morning for more tests. Try to get some sleep. I wanted you to be prepared in case something is wrong."

When he left me to walk down the darkened hallway, I knew the last thing I was going to do was sleep. I should have called Lance, but I didn't. Surely by morning, she would be fine? I slapped my pillow into a more comfortable position and tried to rid myself of anxiety. I made a silent pact with God that night. Christina had to be healthy. She had to be. I couldn't imagine the heartache or the enormity that would soon face us.

At 7:00 a.m. the following morning, Dr. Sessions returned as the sun shone into the room with the promise of spring. And he turned my world upside-down.

"There's no easy way to tell you this. My test results this morning have confirmed my suspicions. Christina definitely has a bowel obstruction and needs emergency surgery because she could not pass meconium. That's the dark green substance forming the first feces of a newborn infant."

"What does that mean?" My fingers gripped the bedding and there was a loud roaring in my ears. I think I stopped breathing for some seconds.

"Since she hasn't passed any meconium in her first twenty-four hours, she's developed progressive abdominal distension. With the history of Cystic Fibrosis in your husband's family, I believe this may be the problem. There could be another disease that could cause the acute blockage called *Hirschsprung's*, but Cystic Fibrosis would be the lesser of the health conditions. Basically, she can't poop."

The rest of the medical jargon that sifted through my world was hazy as I clutched my throat and stared at him. Despite appreciating the sympathy I saw in his freckled face, I couldn't speak. I kept swallowing the large lump in my throat and shook my head against his words. I remember staring at his face as if memorizing the contours of his chin, the high cheek bones and the freshly-shaved face. His white jacket appeared slightly rumpled. His eyes were sad.

"Do you understand what I'm telling you?"

"Not really, but the surgery can fix it?" My voice shook.

"It's a condition called *Meconium Ileus* and there's no time to lose. She must be transferred to Doernbecker Hospital in Portland immediately for surgery."

I dropped my head back onto the pillow and stared at the ceiling. The foreign words multiplied through my head. Fairydust dimmed.
"How will she get there? When will she go? Can I see her first? Can I go with her?" I blurted the questions and held my breath.

"Yes, you can see her first and no, you can't go with her. You're too vulnerable just out of delivery. Can your husband drive her up there today? The doctors will clear her bowel and we will go from there. Do you have any questions?"

"My husband's driving a log truck somewhere east of here and I have no way of contacting him." Fighting panic, my mind tossed around for others. Linda lived in Albany and my parents were in Portland. I was smack between the two cities and too much time would be lost. I took a deep breath. "I feel fine, just a little sore. I want to go with her. Please?" I reached for his hand that rested on the side of my bed.

Dr. Sessions patted my fingers and shook his head. "I'll send the nurse in to talk with you and you can give her the names and numbers of anyone who can rush her to Portland. Fast. The surgeon will be waiting for her arrival. A nurse will accompany your baby with the driver."

My stomach churned with fear. I played every argument in my head repeatedly. My pillow was drenched with tears. I grabbed my robe and padded down to the nurse's station. Susan the nurse, pushed the phone toward me with a look of sadness on her face. I thanked her and dialed Lance's boss, hoping he could call Lance on the truck radio. It was Sunday. Nobody answered. My mind screamed.

I had to make the call. It was my daughter's only chance and I hated the thought. Swallowing my animosity, I dialed the number with shaking fingers. Christina's life hung in the balance and I knew I had no other choice.

As the phone rang, I worded my frantic appeal. My voice was strangely calm. "I need you, Shelley. Christina needs a ride to OHSU. Fast."

And without hesitation, my nemesis responded, "I'm on my way."

I stood there with all the nurses waiting for answers. I'd set pride aside and held the phone in disbelief. It was as if the horror that Shelley had caused in my life had been erased with that one phone call. She'd felt my need as a mother. I put my hands over my face and wept.

Susan, my kind nurse, rushed to my side and led me back to the room. "Stop this, missy. Don't give up before the battle is fought," she said.

I stopped to look at her, guessing she thought I cried because of the fear settling around my heart and mind about Christina instead of my relief at Shelley's response.

She pushed me into my bed and pulled the covers around me. "You just stay put and I'll find a little someone to put your heart at ease," she whispered as she tucked me in. "Barbara is getting the incubator ready and we will watch for your friend to arrive."

Within minutes, I was holding Christina, swaying to music only I could hear. I kissed her velvety cheeks and touched her soft head. I didn't know what a heart full of love felt like until then. She clutched my finger and stared at me, as she had the day before. So trusting. Vulnerable. Blink. Blink. Blink. Fairydust.

Shelley walked into my hospital room. She had no make-up on her face, hair barely brushed. She'd thrown her clothing on, barely resembling the woman I'd watched through my kitchen window for months. We stared at one another wordlessly, each feeling the sorrow and relief for different reasons. When she sat beside me, I burst into tears again. All the sadness, anger and bitterness washed away as she gripped my fingers. I felt something had changed.

Shelley's blue eyes were moist, her features were strained and her chin trembled. "They're placing Christina into an incubator bed and a nurse is riding with us. She said you can walk as far as the elevator. I am so sorry, so sorry for…"

Her empathetic smile thawed my seesaw thoughts. "Thank you for getting here so fast and that you're willing to…." My voice broke.

"Shhh… I'm glad I can help. You must know that." She placed a finger to her lips. "I'll get her to OHSU as fast as I can."

Ten minutes later, a nurse took Christina from my arms and placed her inside a small glass-type infant carrying case. An incubator? It didn't look like one to me. The tiny lump was covered in blankets and I could barely see the small pink face and incredible blue eyes.

The nurse struggled to keep her face a mask of detachment, but lost the fight; her eyes reflected sorrow. She turned to me and Shelley with a nod of her head on the way out of the room.

"Ready?"

I touched the side of the glass before running my fingers along the length of it. In a heartbeat's time, I was standing at the nurse's station across from the elevator. Shelley punched the button, the doors opened and the nurse stepped inside to join her with her precious cargo. The incubator bed looked like a puppy crate one carried onto an airplane, only so much more. My baby was less than two days old.

Time stood still afterward. I closed my eyes, squeezed them shut.

"Hey, kiddo, you didn't think I'd let you sit here feeling sorry for yourself, did you?" The voice whispered close to my ear.

"Sally." I felt her arms around me instantly. "Thank God you're here. I was going nuts being alone." I pointed to the chair and she pulled it close.

"Shelley roared into my driveway this morning and pounded on my front door...she was talking fast, but I pieced together what happened. She knew I'd want to be with you. She said Lance was working and you couldn't find him." Sally plumped my pillow and rubbed my arm. "Maybe there may be some good inside of that woman after all."

I looked at her and couldn't stop the tears.

"I called your Mom before I left, but one of your brothers said she and Ellen were already on their way, so they don't know what's going on. They should arrive soon, so I'll stay until they get here. My Dad has the boys, but he doesn't like having them long." She rolled her eyes.

"Thanks, Sally." I had no other words.

"Remember, the doctors are specialists and if Christina is anything like her mother, she's a fighter. Remember that!"

"Well your timing is incredible. I was losing myself. Lance hasn't returned my call yet. I dread telling him because he will freak out when I tell him about her surgery and CF and..."

"Take it easy, kiddo. Try to relax. Getting yourself worked up isn't going to help anything. What is he going to do, hit you?"

Despite crying like a water spout, I had to agree. Lance had never hit me. Maybe he would control his temper and listen this time...be supportive. He was a father now. That had to mean something, I reasoned. Before the thought finished, a freckle-faced nurse about my age tapped on the door frame and signaled me toward the nurse's station.

"There's a phone call for you. I think it's your hubby," she whispered.

I caught my breath. Sally winked at me and we walked to the telephone. Before I had said more than hello, Lance's questions bombarded me.

"What's wrong? Why did you call my boss? You knew I'd be in to see you tonight…Your message sounded weird."

Forcing calmness I didn't feel, I took a deep breath before telling him what had happened; the doctors' orders, Shelley's arrival, Christina's departure and the possibility of Cystic Fibrosis. That did it.

"Hey! Where do you get this Cystic Fibrosis shit?"

I couldn't answer.

"Are you still there? I said, where do you..?"

"I heard you, Lance! Do you think I'd make up this story? I'm just telling you what I know."

It was his turn to be silent, and then he said, "I'll call again to find out what the doctor says and I'll come see you later." He hung up.

I remember shaking so badly that I sagged against Sally. She took the phone from me and replaced it. Sally had heard it all. In fact, probably everyone within ten feet had heard him. As soon as we retraced our steps back to my room, I burst into tears again. I wanted to cover my head with the covers without speaking to anyone and hide from the world.

"I want to call Lance every dirty word I've heard since first grade."

That brought me back to reality and we laughed. When my sister-in-law Linda, who'd lost her first child to the dreaded disease years earlier, walked into my room, Sally kissed me and left us.

"Now it's my turn, Lin."

"What?" Her face creased into a frown. "I heard the nurses talking about a baby and surgery…"

"CF. Christina is probably being prepped right now at OHSU."

"No, please no…not CF." The air seemed to rush out of her and the look of pain on her face matched my own. I knew she was remembering her infant son's surgery and subsequent death. Cystic Fibrosis.

I thought our combined tears were going to melt us right into the floor. Sitting on my bed and holding my hand, she tried to give me hope, though I knew her heart was breaking. Watching her sweet face, I read love, sadness, and her complete understanding. Her own tragedy lay mirrored in her expressive face.

"When Duane died, they didn't know as much about CF as they do now. Remember the disease was pretty much unknown in the early 1960's. They waited too long to operate. With Christina, there's a better chance. The doctors know more and it's been almost seven years."

"How could I have underestimated the possibility of CF?"

We talked for another hour until Linda saw my mother and godmother Ellen walk down the hallway toward us. Linda's face crumpled when she caught my mother's eye. "Your Mom and Ellen are here."

I closed my eyes tightly. How could I face them without falling to pieces the minute their faces appeared inside the door? How funny life is. Wasn't it just yesterday Mom and Ellen were admiring my 6th grade school picture? Those two best of friends were my pillars of strength. How I needed them, but I didn't really want to talk to anyone. The only people I could depend on for news were the nurses down the hall.

Mom read the anguish on Linda's face before they entered my room.

"What on earth?"

"Honey, what…?"

My words spilled out in a torrent.

My Mom threw her arms around me and I clung to her. "Let's get this straight. They took the baby? Shelley drove Christina to OHSU?

...Shelley?" She repeated the name in disbelief because she knew the woman and the story behind my problems.

"You haven't heard anything from the doctors yet? Let's try to calm down, get a grip on this. Where is Lance?"

The question hung in the air. "He's working and I don't want him here now anyway, Mom."

My Mom's face turned red with anger. She looked at Ellen. Neither woman said a word except to sigh loudly.

"Mom, I really don't care. I just want to hear about the baby. We spoke on the phone and he's angry about CF."

"Oh? *He's* the one who is angry? As if you gave your child this disease on your own? He knows both parents have to carry the gene for a baby to get CF." My Mom's face was stormy.

Ellen reached for my hand, "You know sometimes we're more afraid of what's out there when we don't know what's going on. Give the doctors a chance, honey. Pray a little. We will say a special mass and I know Mary and her sister nuns will too. Please remember things could go well. Come on, where's the spunky girl we've known all our lives?"

Linda kissed my forehead and then she flew down the corridor. My heart hurt for her, for me, my mother and not the least, for Lance too.

Dusk descended on the room. At 6:30 that night, my peace was shattered when the doctor from Doernbecker Hospital called. They were ready to operate. I would not find out until years later that my Dad had spoken to the doctor who held little hope of saving Christina.

"What? I thought she was already in surgery." I panicked again. "Please save my baby's life, yes...yes...please hurry."

I had still not heard from Lance. I could see Mom's face fill with rage every time she glanced at the clock.

"I hate to leave you, honey, but we need to drive home. Please call the minute you hear from the hospital? I wish your husband was here..."

Ellen handed Mom a handkerchief. "Your mascara is smeared all over your cheeks, Neyda." She wiped her own nose and hustled Mom out of my room. I knew they'd kept a brave face for me. They'd probably cry all the way home. I heard Mom say, "I kept Koffee awake for hours last night talking about how beautiful Christina was…is, I mean."

Ellen shushed her. "They're operating on her, not killing her."

"Well, where's my idiot son in law? He should be here!"

"Let's pray about that too, huh?"

They had no idea that their whispered conversation echoed so loudly in the hallway. I was glad to hear the elevator doors close behind them. My head hurt again and then I drifted into a light doze.

I was jerked awake with Lance's loud voice as he entered my room sometime after Mom and Ellen left. His questions pounded at me, demanding answers. "Come on, Pat, there must be something. I haven't been able to drink enough beer to calm me down. Why are you just lying there when our baby is in surgery? I worked all day and there's still no word from Portland?"

"Lance, stop it! I don't need any more shit today."

He stopped to stare at me. Then he laughed. "You're right. I'm an ass." He reached over and caressed my cheek. He held my hand and we sat that way for a long time and then we cried. The strange day had taken a toll on both of us.

"I've been a jerk. Let me try to make it up to you? I know Christina will help us find ourselves again…please…?"

I remember nodding, too numb to do otherwise.

By midnight, we were told, "Surgery is over and she is still alive." Minutes later, the nurse read the report to us. "Dr. Collis confirmed the diagnosis of *Meconium Ileus* and proceeded to surgically open, clear and repair the bowel. Prior to closing the peritoneal layer, a gastrostomy tube was placed in the curvature using the Stamm Technique. A malacot catheter was brought out through a separate stab wound and the last purse-string suture was used to attach it to the underside of the peritoneum next to the wound."

I groaned and shook my head.

More words tumbled out of her mouth. "At the end of the procedure, Christina had a hypothermia and was apneic for fifteen minutes, but responded well to a sodium bicarbonate infusion and received plasma during the procedure."

"Hypothermia?"

"An abnormally low body temperature, but they warmed her up."

"And apneic?" The words stuck in my throat. I pressed my fist into my belly to try to soothe the knots.

She hesitated. "Apneic means a temporary suspension of breathing called infant apnea, like adults with sleep apnea. The doctor's report says Christina tolerated the procedure well. That's good news."

Good news? She was alive. But she hadn't breathed properly for fifteen minutes. Brain damage? I exploded into panic mode as my thoughts crashed through my mind and reverberated around my head. Blockage. Weakness. Rectal thermometer. Intestinal abnormality. Cystic Fibrosis. My heart started pounding again. When sobs rose toward my throat, the brightness of yesterday dimmed.

"Get some sleep. You're right. You have been a jerk. We'll see what tomorrow brings." He looked like a little boy as he walked down the hallway with the burden of our lives weighing him down.

NOTE: As I look back on that day when those elevator doors closed and I returned to my room, I asked myself why an ambulance didn't take Christina to Portland. Why was it imperative that I find someone to drive her to the hospital? It was fifty miles away, but surely an ambulance… When I asked the hospital that question years later when I began to write my memoir, they did not have an answer for me.

CHAPTER SEVEN

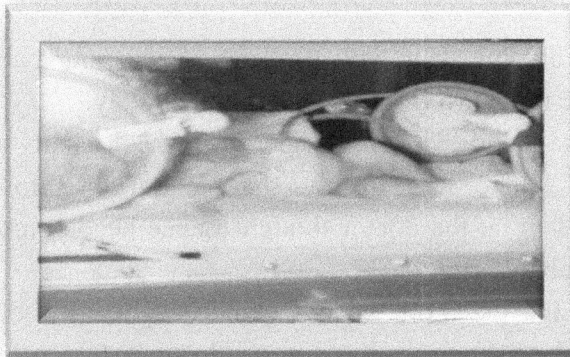

Three days after her birth, I could finally leave the hospital. Christina was still alive. All I could think of was being with her, holding her, kissing her soft cheeks. I wanted to see for myself that my child was truly healing from her surgery. After a hot shower, I squeezed into my black stretch pants and waited for a release from my hospital prison.

Dr. Wood found me there and chuckled when he pulled up a chair. "Well, my girl, you look as ready as I've ever seen anyone."

I tried to smile but I was so wound up, I just nodded.

"I'm sorry about your little one. Have faith. You'll see her soon. I understand the surgery went well, she's resting comfortably this morning and I'm sure you want to get on your way. Your husband is signing papers at the front desk and your mother-in-law is parked at the entrance door. I've signed your release and they're bringing you a wheel chair. Hospital policy and all that stuff," he chuckled again.

I managed a smile that time.

"By the way, I'm sorry I wasn't more knowledgeable about the disease your baby may have. I know you told me months ago about CF and I didn't think it was anything you should worry about. God, I'm sorry. Dr. Sessions specializes in CF here in Salem. How'd you happen to choose him from all the pediatricians here?"

"I let my fingers do the walking through the yellow pages," I quipped. Excitement banked my fears; I couldn't imagine another outcome.

"Well, my dear, you probably saved your baby's life with your choice. He recognized the problem immediately."

Dr. Wood walked beside my wheel chair with Lance to the elevator. Lance was freshly shaved, but his bloodshot eyes spoke volumes. I think the doctor thought Lance needed more help than I did. He was probably right.

At the elevator, when I glanced up from the wheelchair to say goodbye, the look of sorrow on my doctor's face turned my stomach to jelly. Fear washed over me again when he shook his head and then he was gone.

I knew Lance expected me to lean on him, but all I could do was stare at the tiny pink baby booties grasped tightly in my lap. A gift from Sally.

Once in the car, I saw a donut pillow waiting for me. "Thanks for bringing me a pillow to sit on, Neva. With everything else on our minds, you're still practical. It's been so painful to sit. This sure feels good though." My mother-in-law smiled at me as I scrunched down to get comfortable, looking for the right spot.

Our laughter broke the ice. Everyone began talking at once.

The race was on. Christina, here we come, I thought.

She drove me, Lance and Linda the fifty miles to Oregon Health Science University, more aptly called OHSU or the hill because the hospital sits high above the west side of Portland. There were more buildings in the medical complex than I could count.

I sat stiffly beside Lance, who smoked all the way north. He withdrew from the conversation. I knew he was thinking of his deceased siblings. I was positive about that. When we arrived and he tried to help me out of the car, I pulled back from him. I don't know why except some part of me was still angry because we couldn't share what new parents should share. When he saw me hesitate, he smiled sadly before closing the car door to follow us into the hospital.

"Be prepared," he whispered.

"No! I won't give her up without a fight."

Lance grunted in agreement. "I know how you feel, Pat. Don't you think I want to cry and crawl into a hole too? And be alone?"

I answered immediately. "No, you don't know how I feel."

"Life is a bitch." He put a cigarette into his mouth and lit it.

Linda squeezed my hand.

Neva, my mother-in-law didn't say a word. She'd already lost two children to CF and her young son, Roy, fought it daily. I saw her face pucker upand then Lance tossed the cigarette onto the ground.

I saw my childhood friend, Meg, waiting and she guided us into the elevator after our hasty hug. "NICU is on the tenth floor. I have to get back to work, but just follow the signs. I'll be up soon."

Hospital odors collided with my fear after Meg led us toward the glass doors on the neonatal intensive care unit, better known as NICU. Since Meg worked at the hospital, she was a wonderful connection for us. I couldn't have survived those days without her meticulous care and love. She was due to deliver her own child in ten days, but she did not let her bulk slow her down.

As we rounded the corner, I saw Mom waiting for us. I rushed toward her and felt that mother embrace give me the strength I needed. "I was hoping you'd be here, Mom."

"And where did you think I'd be, honey?"

Lance spoke then, a little angry, afraid and very loud. "Where's the baby? Where's the doctor? What's going on?"

Neva turned toward Mom. "Neyda, is something else wrong?"

Everyone began to talk at once. Mom held up a hand. "Meg has been in and out all morning. She's tried to find out as much information as she can and should be back any minute. She's the medical secretary on the next floor. She's already brought me two cups of coffee since she arrived at 7:30 this morning." Mom pointed to the double-glass doors where we read NO ADMITTANCE printed in eight-inch letters. "There. Christina's in there. The nurses rolled her incubator to the window[1] earlier for me to look at her. Meg helped…we are so lucky to have her here."

"Mom. What does she look like since her surgery?"

"Honey, you'll just have to…"

Meg rounded the corner and motioned everyone toward the glass doors. When she knocked, we stared into the large inner confines of the unit. Within minutes, a nurse with a black pony tail, wheeled Christina toward us. When I saw her tiny body with a rubber tube attached to her belly and an IV needle pierced into her ankle, it caught me off guard. The thin glass between us seemed like a mile instead of a quarter inch. She was alive. My arms ached and my milk-heavy breasts throbbed.

---

[1] I didn't know until much later that Mom had taken a photo of Christina that morning because she feared it may be the only one she had. The incubator photo was the only one I had from that time in OHSU.

"Where's the doctor? I want to thank him for saving her." Lance's voice was etched with emotion and he rocked on his feet as he peered inside.

We huddled in the small alcove to stare at our baby through the glass windows. "I can't believe there are so many stitches across her tummy. And what's that little cup taped to the inside of the glass with the long tube? I need to ask the doctor some questions," I whispered.

Suddenly, an exhausted-looking doctor emerged from NICU with a scowl on his face. He threw the glass doors open so hard, I had to jump out of the way. He pulled off his gloves and slapped his thigh before staring at us. "Why in the hell would you permit a child to come into this world with so many odds against her?"

His bluntness and anger stunned us but before we could say a word, he continued, "There is a 90% chance your daughter has Cystic Fibrosis. But then you know about the disease. I've read her chart, so I understand there's a history of the disease riddling your family. At this point, Christina is holding her own." His hair stood up on one side as if he'd been asleep. The white coat was wrinkled, he needed a shave. He didn't wait for an answer. We could have heard a pin drop when he strode off down the hall.

I caved in. "Is he right? Is there a test we could have taken to see if I was a CF carrier? Wait, the doctor told us there is no test. That's not right..." My words trailed off.

Meg was livid and threw her arms around me. "I can't believe Dr. Collis or any doctor would say those things." She wiped tears off her cheeks and led me to a chair.

"Let's only think about Christina. As much as I hated hearing what he said, he may have been right. He was practically asleep on his feet. I don't have room for any more anger right now. I just want to be with my baby." My breasts felt ready to explode since I wasn't nursing my baby, so when Lance turned toward me, I put up a hand to stop him.

He assumed I didn't want him to touch me and turned away.

My mother-in-law began to cry.

My memory of that day still rings brightly because Lance suddenly turned to me and said, "What the hell? I want answers."

Meg wasn't finished. "The doctor has seen too many babies go through the pain of such surgeries, but it's still no excuse to blast you. Don't make excuses for him. There's absolutely no reason for that behavior any time or under any condition."

I ignored Lance. Instead, I slid my fingers along the glass as if I could stroke Christina's skin. She lay so still in the high bed. Soft, pale and helpless, my baby slept as if there wasn't a care in her world. I tried to tune everyone out until Lance touched my arm to get my attention.

"Let me find a nurse who can answer your questions," Meg said as she tried to lift the tenseness between us. She was always the arbiter.

Everyone inside the unit heard Dr. Collis' outburst and they whispered between themselves. When Meg pointed toward one of the nurses, she whispered, "Suzanne, are you Christina's nurse?"

The young woman with the black pony tail nodded and came to the door. After Meg introduced each of us, the nurse smiled.

"I must get back to work. I almost forgot that I have a job," Meg said apologetically and then disappeared.

"I'm sure you have a lot of questions and I will try to answer them all but first, let me explain a few things. Then you can ask your questions, okay? Let's sit down." She led everyone to the benches along the wall.

"She's going to be all right?" Lance's voice was strained.

"Your baby is doing well now. Let's start at the beginning, hmm?" He continued, "I just…"

"Please, let me try to tell you everything I know about your baby and then it will be your turn, agreed?" She smiled at us like we were children. I guess we were.

I took a deep breath. Mom grabbed my hand and I kept my milk-filled chest averted as much as possible. I'd never had that kind of pain and didn't dare let anyone near me.

"As I understand it, Christina didn't pass any meconium in the first twenty-four hours of her life. Infants must do this to have a normal bowel movement. Meconium is a putty-like substance that is in the bowel at birth. And they should pass it shortly after birth. She couldn't. That's why she's here."

"What's that meconium have to do with Cystic…"

Suzanne held up her hand. "You wouldn't remember the name of the operation, but the complications they can cause are frightening. That is the blockage. When she developed the abdominal distension, your pediatrician recognized the problem. He knew surgery was the only thing to save your baby because there was a strong family history of CF on her father's family tree."

Neva stared at the floor and gripped her hands in her lap. I was stunned to see Lance reach over and stroke his mother's fingers. When she looked up, equally surprised, it warmed me. She needed that.

"Dr. Collis specializes in this type of surgery on infants. He had to use a microscope and it's fairly new to the field. We are thrilled to have him here to perform this advanced procedure."

"A first for Christina. She's bringing a lot of firsts for me too. Operating with a microscope is fascinating."

Suzanne smiled. "I see you glancing toward your baby every few seconds and I see the pain on your face too. What you see attached to Christina is practically her lifeline at this point. It looks frightening, I know that. Let me tell you what everything is," Suzanne said as her pony tail bobbed around her shoulder. She stood up and invited us to look inside what she called an isolette.

My mind hummed her name. Christina Marie.

"The gauges along the inside of the isolette help us keep track of her body functions. The tubes you see are for many different things. The large bandage across her lower stomach area is where the surgery was of course. The IV taped to her ankle feeds her antibiotics. The tiny stab wound below her incision was made for that tube's access to her bowel movements." She pointed to the cup taped onto the inside of the glass wall. "The tube empties into that tiny cup because since her surgery, we must catch her solid waste because until the incision in her intestine heals, we can't allow her to have a normal bowel movement. Hence, the catheter. I know she looks totally wired up, but it's all necessary. She's improving every minute. Now, ask your questions." She looked at Lance because he was pacing while she talked to our group.

Now, suddenly everyone was quiet, including Lance. He looked at Suzanne, turned toward Christina and then sat on the bench with his eyes closed. He sagged against the wall and dropped his head.

I looked away because I felt the same way, but refused to let myself sink, sink, sink. I felt my throat close up for a second. "Thanks, Suzanne. I'm sure I'll see a lot of you. You're the only person who has explained this to us so that we understand it."

She smiled. "And you, Momma, need some rest too." She nodded and returned to the unit, patting the top of Christina's bed along the way.

Christina's skin was tinged with the orange solution from surgery. I looked at the tube dangling from her stomach, the big bandage, the IV and cup taped to the bed. I let out a long breath. Time. Now, we need time.

"I have to admit the surgery on my first grandchild looks frightening. I feel better after her explanation. Don't you think so too?" My Mom sank down on the bench near Lance.

I sat down beside her. When she put an arm around me, I flinched. "My breasts hurt so much, Mom. I think they're going to explode. They are so swollen and feel hard as a rock."

"We should get you home and put ice packs on them. That happened to me when Michael was born and I couldn't nurse him..."

Suzanne returned, waved to us and pushed Christina's isolette away from the window. I think she knew that was the only way to get me away from the hospital for some rest.

"I wanted to hold her. But I know it's impossible with all those tubes hooked up between her and the bed. I can't go home without her."

"We need to go home." Lance's blue eyes were glazed with tears. He wiped them with a flick of his hand as he guided me into the elevator.

I couldn't believe what I heard. "I am not leaving my daughter. What is wrong with you? We just got here." I knew my voice was shaking. I wanted to hit him. Hard. "I'm staying to bring her home."

"Home? Or to your parent's house?"

I stared at Lance without answering.

He didn't argue, still uncertain of the status between us. We were like lost children. The day had changed me, strengthened me, and killed me just a little. And then he left without me.

§

The next morning, I saw a man wheel Christina to the NICU window in front of us. I was a little dumbstruck. The doctor... I squeezed my fingers into the palm of my hand, took a breath. I wanted to punch him, but also hug him for saving Christina.

He opened the glass doors to join us in the hallway and looked at me and Mom. "Good morning, ladies. I know I didn't make a good impression yesterday. Forgive me for acting like an ass. It grieves me to see these babies born with a disease that I can't heal. Her color is very good and she's alert and active."

I mumbled something, but I can't remember the words.

"As you can see," he continued, "she's being medicated with an IV and she's gaining strength. In fact, Suzanne tells me she's kicking and moving around in there, probably mad as hell because she's trussed up like a Thanksgiving turkey."

I was stunned to see him lean against the cream-colored wall nonchalantly. He looked like the same doctor; the voice was the same, but...

Mom's face mirrored my surprise.

"Each day you should see improvements and I'll make sure you're told of the changes daily. I see a Portland phone number in your file, so I assume you'll be in the city for a while?"

"Yes." That's the only word that peeped out of me.

He touched my shoulder and finished with, "I'm hopeful." And then he left us to stare after him as his white coat went around the corner.

Mom looked at me and we burst into silent laughter.

"I know. Incredible, huh?"

The next two hours, I watched my daughter breathe while I pressed my nose against the glass. Each day, I positioned myself near the window and a nurse wheeled Christina toward me. Her small body was still smudged with orange dye, riddled with stitches to hold her belly together and a tiny bucket was tethered to her so she could poop. I was assured that once her intestine was healed, it would be removed so she could fill a diaper on her own. Her thin legs kicked and her arms swung around like a pendulum.

I met Dr. Julia Grach, the head of the Cystic Fibrosis Clinic. I liked her immediately. She stood barely five feet tall, had dark skin and big brown eyes. She was good friends with my friend Meg, who told me Julia Grach was a Samoan princess who left her island country to be a doctor.

She began to explain the impact of the disease I knew little about. "As you know by now, Cystic Fibrosis is a hereditary disease affecting the mucus-secreting glands and the sweat glands of the body. It takes its toll on many organs, particularly the lungs and the pancreas. Normally, mucus performs a valuable protective and lubricating function. In the CF patient, it becomes thick and sticky, clogging and prohibiting the normal functions of the pancreas, intestines, salivary glands, and especially the lungs. Because CF patients appear to die from pneumonia, asthma, malnutrition and chronic diarrhea, the disease was not identified until 1938."

I stared at the short woman and cringed at the word die. She squeezed my arm when she saw my reaction. I felt cold all over as the enormity pressed against my heart.

Dr. Grach said, "Christina can have a normal life with special care. I will teach you everything and set up a respiratory therapist to work with you. She will need medications, sleep in a mist tent and she will need to be clapped three times a day."

"Clapped?" I was learning an entire new language.

Her words gathered steam as she smiled at me and said, "That is what we call postural drainage, which is chest physiotherapy. We will teach you everything before this little one goes home with you." She looked at her file. "A chronic cough, recurrent lung infections and shortness of breath will be part of her life. Thick mucus will plug her airways and that's what sets her up for infections. The pancreas suffers from the same kind of plugging. Without the enzymes it produces, food is not absorbed. Much of this is correctable by taking digestive enzymes along with vitamins and minerals. Her forehead tastes salty; that's a sign to diagnose the disease."

Her words rushed over me but I also felt a kindred connection. A germ of hope crept up my spine. Despite the shock of learning Christina had CF and feeling inadequate to give her proper care, the doctor seemed to think I could do it all. And I wanted to believe her.

When Lance called that night to say, "I am too tired to come up, so I'll be up there at the weekend," I realized I hadn't missed him or his phone calls. But I also knew my dream to move to Portland, get a job and raise Christina alone was gone. Cystic Fibrosis now controlled our lives. I turned to Plan B, a shadowy future to worry about later. For now, Christina was my only priority.

In the first days after Christina's surgery, I would sit by the isolette, still stunned by the unfamiliar surroundings. In the weeks to come, life outside the hospital would take on illusory qualities, while the intensive care unit would become my real world. I would measure my days in the minutes I stood outside the glass doors staring into the little isolette that was her first home. Despite only two feet separating us, she was beyond reach. We stared at her through the glass and Christina gazed at us curiously.

One morning, the nurse Suzanne, met me with a smile on her face as she gently lifted her tiny patient, ever careful not to dislodge the IV stuck into her ankle. I watched Suzanne's fingers weave through the wires and tubing to hold Christina gently away from the flat bedding. We all shared laughter when she kicked sharply and surprised us.

"She's very active today. There must have been some vitamins lacing her antibiotics," she said with a laugh. After pushing Christina close to the glass windows for me and my mother, she returned to her other duties. I noticed she was never too far away that she couldn't listen for her cries.

I watched Christina's little arms and legs flail so wildly that the IV needle flew out of her ankle. Blood spurted over her. I knocked wildly on the glass to get attention. Suzanne ran toward us, saw the problem and pushed the door open a few inches. "Don't worry. She's all right. This may take a while. Why don't you two go down to the lunchroom for coffee and come back in about half an hour?"

Mom had to pull me away from the alcove.

When we returned, Suzanne walked into the hallway. "We moved the IV. Your little one is too rowdy for her own good. I guess she just wants out. She's awake most of the time now, although she's sleeping and eating normally. Now, don't get upset when you see her."

"Why? What do you mean...?" I stuttered.

"It's just that...well, you saw her earlier. She's raring to get out of her cage and she can't. So, we had to place the IV into her head. I know. I can see you cringe. It will look worse than it is, but it's a normal procedure. Please remember the medicine flowing into her system is very important. No matter where we put it, right?"

I tried to prepare myself. I saw the bandage on her ankle. The wires were still there. Tubes were intact. Then I caught my breath. They'd shaved off her golden hair.

Mom put her arm around me. "It's just hair."

"She doesn't seem to notice there's a needle stuck in her head. I feel like I'm strangling. Can't they see I just want to hold her? Feel her close? Touch her? My brain is screaming all the time. Waiting, waiting to have her close, pretending she's a normal baby. I feel like the doctors and nurses are talking to me like I'm a kewpie doll, not an adult, her mother. Damn!"

"Honey, I'm sure that isn't the case at all."

"I want to hold her though. What could it hurt to let me do that? I fear for her life and I want to..." I couldn't say the words or tell Mom that I worried that she might die without my holding her warm body again. How could I say that when I hated admitting it to myself? And where was Lance in all this? Every time I tried to talk to him about what was happening with our baby, he clammed up, changed the subject and lit another cigarette. I can still hear him exhale and blow out that hefty stream of ugly smoke.

Mom was quiet before answering me. "I know. Life isn't always fair. Some say God has a reason for everything, but you know how I feel about that? I've asked myself many times how God could let this happen. But, it has...now let's stop panicking. You're doing well. The ice helped your boobs and Christina's active with good color. Let's go home."

Each day brought something new to celebrate. Gaining an ounce in weight. A smile. My breasts finally dried up. By day number seven, Christina had her first bowel movement and a bottle of sugar water mixed with milk formula. I still couldn't hold her, but we were making progress. She was now in a tiny bed. No more incubator.

The nurses cheered as I arrived that morning. Suzanne said, "She pooped in her diaper!" I still laugh today when I think of it. That day, the old adage of don't sweat the small stuff changed to celebrate the small stuff.

The daily hospital routine didn't vary. The NICU nurses checked babies, worked around doctors and interns. And they kept an eye trained on the glass visitor doors for parents who ached to see their babies just like I did that first day and the weeks that followed. Some trudged through their regimen with an eye on the clock while others raced with an efficiency I marveled at. Suzanne was becoming our best friend away from home.

Mom was still working full time, keeping house and raising my brothers. The chaos in her life did not stop her from visiting her grandchild. I am unsure if I could have lived through those days without her. My second visit to see Christina each day was when Mom drove me up the hill after dinner each evening. It was then that I explained the daily changes and she turned into a gushing grandmother in front of my eyes.

Mom tapped on the window. "Look at those tiny fingers, honey. Just like when you were small. It's been twenty-two years, but it seems like yesterday. I can't stop looking at her." She squeezed my arm. "And I'm just the grandma. You must be over the moon."

I smiled as warmth consumed me. I loved Mom so much. Since we were only sixteen years apart, we were also good friends. We liked it that way and it seemed as if the generation gap wasn't that far off at all. I wanted that closeness between me and my own daughter. I must. It was too fragile to miss. I smiled at Mom and tried to imagine myself beside Christina when she was twenty-two. The image was blurry, so I shook it off.

~

That night, Lance called. "I can't come to Portland this weekend."

I sighed loudly, told him about the IV fiasco and explained the postural drainage to him.

He responded, "I don't know if I can do it."

When I heard his negative responses about Christina's needs to maintain her health, I didn't care if he drove up to visit or not. The mantra I'd repeated for months about Christina being my baby seemed truer as each day dawned. But what could I do?

As the days turned into nearly two weeks, the regimen was set. Christina stayed inside. I stood outside and looked in. I'd make faces at her and she would stare at me with those huge blue eyes. The days blurred into each other. I lost track of time, people and myself. I prayed.

One day, Meg found me sitting in the chair by the glass. She stood there, hugging her big belly with the palms of her hands. She lovingly stroked it over and over again.

"I am giving my baby up for adoption." She whispered and sat down beside me. "There are no words to tell you that seeing Christina and you here…knowing we've been friends since we were ten years old, I couldn't keep this secret[2] any longer."

My body flushed hot and I stared at her. It would be some days before the full story burst from her. For now, she was here for me.

"How are you holding up?" She smiled at me.

Trying to set aside her shocking statement for now, I saw that she had no intention of saying any more about it. "I'm told Christina's doing well and I know they have their rules, but why can't I go inside to hold her? My head aches, my stomach is in knots. Every time a doctor comes near me, I expect he's going to let me go inside. When, when, when…?

Meg hugged me. "Remember what I've been telling you. I check on her every day before I go home and every morning when I arrive. I know you're under a horrible strain and I'm sorry. I wish I had some magical words for you, but the doctors and nurses know what they're

---

[2] This is Meg's story, not mine, so I will not include it here. However, after much drama, she chose to keep her baby who grew up to be my goddaughter and is now a successful pediatrician in Washington state.

doing. I know it's hard. Dr. Grach is very smart and caring…like they are her own kids. She has a huge file on Christina already."

I felt guilty because Meg obviously had her own problems, but she still worked behind the scenes for me and my baby too.

"You'll hold her soon, I'm sure. Leave the timing to them, Patricia," she said as she nodded toward the glass doors in front of us.

"I'll try…but it's agonizing. It's hard to think straight in here. The halls close in on me every day. You know, it's been ages since we just talked. Why don't you come to dinner at Mom's? She and Dad love you and since you live alone…" I didn't want to make her uncomfortable, but we definitely needed to talk about her problem.

She looked pleased. "Okay, what time?"

"Come after work. I need a diversion; I spend too much time feeling sorry for myself. I know Mom and Dad are tired of hearing me whine. Your company would be good…it will probably shut me up …"

Meg chuckled. "Christina is beautiful. She's going to be okay, I just know it. You are so lucky to have this child. Don't let the little things get in the way. When is Lance coming up? I haven't seen him much."

"I haven't either." I looked away from her. "He's working and too busy to drive up. Maybe this week end. Life isn't good between us."

"Oh, honey. I'm sorry." Her eyes filled up.

"I planned to move to Portland to get a job, but Lance didn't know my plans. Now, with Christina sick…" My chin trembled.

"What life is giving us, huh? There are answers out there, let's keep looking for them. Listen to the doctors; they have Christina's best interest at heart. Please? I better get back to work. I'll see you later. Be sure to call Neyda so she knows I'm coming. I don't want to just drop by and surprise her." When she returned to her office, the hallway resumed its silence. A couple stood by the window to stare at their sick baby. I saw the man reach for his wife's hand and then put his arm around her. I envied their closeness. Yes, I felt sorry for myself for so many reasons.

CHAPTER EIGHT

Changes were in the air. On day number ten, March 25, I arrived at the NICU to see all the nurses grinning at me through the glass. I was invited inside for the first time. Impatient with the desire to hold and touch my daughter, I stood at the sink several minutes to perform the ritual scrubbing with antiseptic soap as they instructed me. There was a sign above the sink that read "Waiting is the law of life, the measure of love." It brought a smile. Right?

After I was bacteria-free, the nurse led me to a rocking chair and placed Christina into my arms. I nearly fainted with pleasure. She was so light and I was so afraid of dropping her that I held her like a piece of glass. No more tubes and wires. The shape of her face, the shape of her slender arms and fingers reminded me of a little doll. Everything was miniature.

I silently questioned my ability to care for this tiny infant. There was no night and day in the hospital, the bright lights never allowed darkness to descend. I knew darkness would be waiting for me in Salem. And there would be silence. No monitors would ring, and no nurse would rescue me when I needed saving. But I knew there was no one to love her the way I did. I rocked her and caressed her tiny body through the soft blanket. The nurses' voices grew blurry as I gazed at my baby through tears, a curtain filled with raindrops.

Suzanne gave me a small bottle of milk and nodded for me to feed Christina. Yes, it is the small things that make up the miracles. "We are trying to calculate how many digestive enzymes to give her and if she continues to improve, you may be feeding this little one at home soon."

All I could do was grin.

Mom and Ellen arrived. We pushed the bassinette to the window.

This time, I was on the inside looking out.

Three days later, Lance and I met with Dr. Grach together in the CF Clinic. She explained the medical advances being made for CF patients. Lance was silent during our visit and didn't ask many questions. Me? That's all I did was ask questions. About everything. I wanted to learn how to take care of this little miracle. I couldn't guess why Lance was so quiet.

The doctor asked me to call the Cystic Fibrosis Foundation because there were funds to pay for some of the medical equipment Christina would require when we took her home.

Once Lance and I arrived at Mom and Dad's house, the truth about his silence emerged. He pulled me aside and said, "I already lost Ronnie and Loretta when they were little. I don't want to love Christina like I did my brother and sister because when she dies…"

I was shocked. "Stop it."

"We have to face reality. She may not live long."

"I said stop it." My heart rate bumped up a notch and I couldn't look at him during my brother's birthday party. When Carl blew out his thirteen candles, I stared at Lance, who studiously stared at the floor. When he left early the next morning, I was glad to see him go.

Christina was still losing weight. They couldn't calculate how many enzyme granules to give her to retain proteins. Without the proper amount in her system, her milk passed through her like a sieve. So, we would not be taking her home any time soon.

In the mix of the craziness of my days and Christina's healing process, Meg delivered a healthy baby girl. My parents helped her, adding adventure to our sometimes-sad days. My brothers helped her move to an apartment. Mom taught her how to mother her child. I still remember the first morning she came downstairs. She looked like she had a hangover and she didn't drink much alcohol.

When pancreatic granules were given to Christina from an eye dropper instead of her milk bottle, Christina neared her birth weight; she now weighed five pounds, ten ounces.

"Postural drainage," the doctor explained. "You will need to clap her several times a day after her breathing treatments. Her lungs have too much mucus. She needs a special milk blend called Nutramigen. We'll cut a hole in the bottle's nipple so the enzymes can slide through the thickened milk. I want her to get used to that before you go home. No more eye dropper…And then her postural drainage can begin to get out that stubborn mucus.

I rolled the words over in my mind. It sounded scary, but I had researched the therapy and my parents were willing to help me. The thought of returning to Salem did not make me happy, but I admitted it was the only way. I hoped I could teach Lance everything the nurses taught me. But I was wrong.

When I outlined her therapy to Lance, he said, "You can do that since you'll be home all day. I'll be working by the time you bring her home from the hospital. She'll be used to you. I can try a couple of times, but…"

My mind went crazy with emotional thoughts. My face must have shown how our lives had become daunting, nerve-wracking. He studied me before kissing me on the cheek and then he drove back to Salem. He'd been there for thirty minutes.

~

CHAPTER NINE

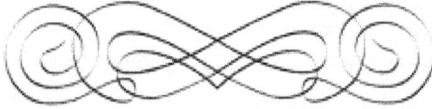

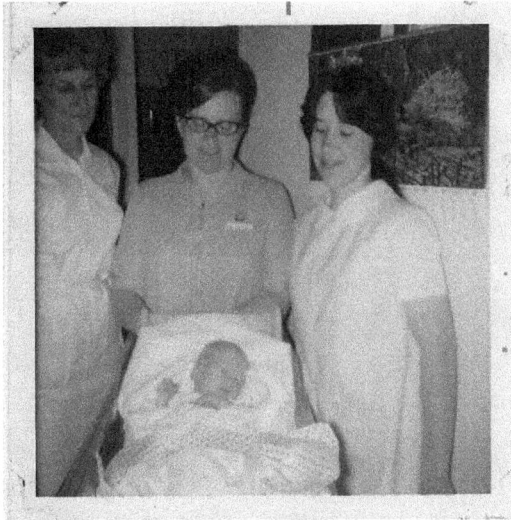

The days were long, tumbling one upon the other like dominoes. Meg and I became close once again, renewing our childhood friendship, listening to each other's woes. And the quiet times together seemed to bridge the gap between my frustration and our uncertainties.

When Christina's lungs became more congested, her physical therapy began in earnest. Dr. Grach had hoped the clogged lungs part of CF would not manifest itself until she was older and stronger, but that wish was not to be. As it was, I was relieved that it happened while still in the hospital; I didn't want to wonder what to do home all alone.

I read everything I could about this disease and maintaining CF children's health. As I write this, I found the best encapsulated definition of Christina's disease written by James McIntosh: Cystic fibrosis is a hereditary disease that affects the lungs and digestive system. The body produces thick and sticky mucus that can clog the lungs and obstruct the pancreas. Cystic fibrosis (CF) can be life-threatening, and people with the condition tend to have a shorter-than-normal life span. Sixty years ago, many children with CF died before reaching elementary school age. However, advances in treatment mean that people with CF often live into their 30s, 40s, and beyond. There is currently no cure for CF. It affects some 30,000 people in the United States with around 1,000 new cases diagnosed each year; 75% are children under the age of 2 years.

So far, the therapist was in charge, but I knew it would soon be my turn. When the scale went over five pounds again, everyone knew her pancreatic enzymes were finally working. The postural drainage was also working. However, my baby was so exhausted from being thumped on by the therapist while holding her in various positions across her lap, Christina was nearly too tired to suck the milk from her bottle afterward.

Learning how to do postural drainage therapy was frightening. I don't know if it was because I thought I would hurt her or if I was afraid I could not learn how to do it properly. But, day twenty one arrived and there was no more thinking about it.

My turn. The respiratory therapist showed me how to hold Christina on my lap with her head angled downward. I could only use three fingers for now, instead of cupping my hand over her lungs since she was so small. The point was to clap her lungs to force excess mucus up so she would be forced to cough. I was afraid of hurting her, but the thrill of finally holding her in my arms eased my trepidation.

The thick enzymes clotted up the bottle's nipple and it was hard on her, but she kept sucking until it emptied, slow but sure. I stared at her in wonder, thankful that she was a fighter. Her tiny fingers wrapped around mine and I couldn't stop tracing my own across her head, cheek and arms. When she was awake, she stared at me like a little bird, unsure of what was going to happen next. Her baby smell was mixed in the many hospital smells, but to me, the baby smell lingered above it all. I held her as close to my cheek as I could in between the feedings and postural drainage.

And I clapped her every day when I arrived until Suzanne whispered on day twenty seven to me, "Maybe she can go home soon."

My heart rocketed. And then she must have seen the lack of confidence cross my face because she laughed. "You can do it," she promised.

I started packing up when I got back to Mom's, sure that she would be driving me and Christina to Salem soon. We talked deep into the night about my worries, my hopes, my fears and so much more. She and Dad knew my life was a crazy roller coaster of emotions, but they continued to treat me like an adult and I was grateful. There were days when I wished they would just tell me what to do, like when I was a child. But, the next minute I was glad they were there regardless of my choices.

The next day at the hospital was a bust. I knew it the minute I arrived at the hospital and entered the NICU unit with my arms still red from the ten-minute scrubbing.

"Between the new formula and the digestive enzymes, Christina's bottom looks like raw meat. She's active, smiling and drinking just fine. She's gaining weight. She's starting to cough up that muck. But her butt is on fire." Suzanne listed everything in a rush of words.

I tried not to cry. Instead, I watched as she changed her diaper and I saw what she meant. Her bum looked like a terrible sunburn and reminded me of my burned legs the previous year in Monterey. It was difficult to stop depression from rearing its ugly head. When Lance called me that evening, I flooded our conversation with tears.

"When can you bring Christina home?"

"Not yet," I sighed loudly and wiped my cheeks with a hand.

"Well, I won't come up this weekend then." He was drunk. I heard him expelling deep inhalations of his cigarette smoke.

The man was very complicated and I was glad he wasn't in the room with me. I rarely raised my voice but often wanted to yell at him. Maybe if I'd done just that, things might have been different. But that old disease to please crippled me and I said, "Okay."

I was exhausted and his words shot me backward. I knew that despite his punching my emotional buttons, I could not care for Christina alone. I couldn't go back to work. I couldn't expect Mom and Dad to raise my child. They had already raised me and three sons. It was their turn to have a life. I had to get my mind right and accept Lance with his insecurities. We had to make it work. Despite his selfishness turning me inside out, I knew he was afraid. And for Christina's sake, I told myself I could face anything. So, I didn't yell at him that night as hurt filled me up.

During the month, we saw each other one day and two weekends.

I pulled on my big girl shoes.

I focused on my daughter and prayed.

CHAPTER TEN

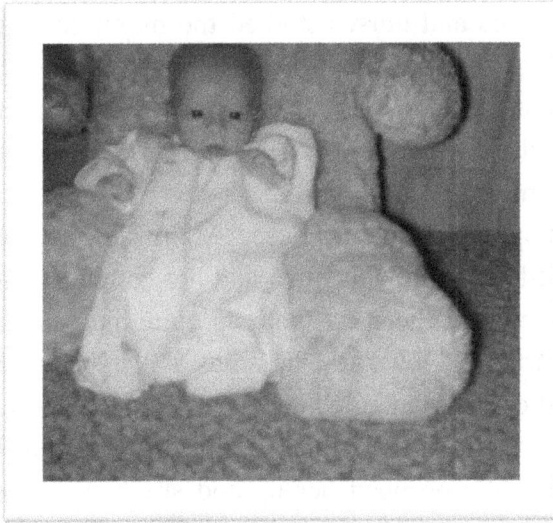

The day we had ceased to believe would ever arrive was imminent. Christina was twenty eight days old and we were taking her home. To Salem. To Lance.

Mom couldn't stop smiling when we arrived at the hospital unit after we received the call for our red-letter day. The nurses invited her inside the NICU with me. She and I went through the detailed hand and arm scrubbing routine. I dressed Christina in real clothes, fed her a bottle with milk infused with enzymes and handed her over into her grandmother's arms for the first time. We were both shaking with emotion and wiping tears off our faces. The nurses did the same. It was a bittersweet day for them too. Christina had become their family.

We joked with the nurses and said goodbye to all the babies who had shared our baby's disinfectant-filled room. I felt tears develop deep within me as I looked at the nurses who had filled my life with grace over the past month. Unconventional friendships maybe, but for me, so real. I had sat by the window of the incubator for two weeks twice a day and watched the tiny, scrawny, beautiful four pound body cling to life while the army of doctors and nurses studied the monitors, adjusted tubes and needles and shook their heads. I had prayed like I'd never prayed before. I'd dreamed of a little blonde-haired girl, saw her first smile and waited with everyone else for her weight reach the magic five-pound number so she could go home.

"First stop, we go to our house," Mom said. In northeast Portland, visitors streamed in. Although Ellen and her daughter, Tina, had seen the baby through the glass, there was nothing quite like holding the squirming infant in their arms. It felt like Christmas as I tracked Christina with my eyes as each set of arms snuggled her.

It was Easter time and there was a massive yellow stuffed bunny waiting for her. We propped her up and she had her first photo shoot. Everyone took turns until I became jittery because Lance was waiting.

"Okay, enough pictures, it's time to drive south."

My head was full of instructions. There was milk and her medicines in the car. Her room in Salem was waiting with piles of baby clothes, diapers and her anxious father. I promised myself we would create a different life, one with laughter, a family unit and maybe a real connection with Lance. I have always been a dreamer and that day was no different.

In those days, infants did not have the safety of car seats, so I held her in my arms as Mom drove us to Salem.

I squeezed the poor little girl too tightly. "I probably have too many blankets on her. Dr. Grach said to be careful so Christina doesn't get a cold. Her lungs are vulnerable because of the thick mucus. She's so little. How can she cough it up? Those tiny little coughs she gives me when I clap her hardly bring up that stuff…I wonder if…" I stopped when Mom chuckled.

"Stop it." Mom stared at Christina and then looked back to the road. Her lips twitched. My teenage brother Carl sat in the back seat, enamored with his little niece.

When sweat started dripping down Christina's forehead, I loosened everything. I had a lot to learn. Mom knew it too. The struggle was just beginning, especially since my single-motherhood plans had been tossed out the window with her diagnosis.

That first evening was both magical and frightening. Mom moved around like a robot, unpacking the car, making a roast for dinner, cleaning the kitchen, washing dishes. She wanted to give me and Lance time with Christina, but I knew she was itching to get her arms around her. One would think after a month filled with lights, noises, nurses and all the events leading up to our bringing her home that she would have been cranky. But, she was quiet, curious and smiled at the least provocation. Her Uncle Carl talked to her soothingly and turned giddy when she gave him a toothless grin.

That night, she slept by our bed in the small bassinette that had belonged to Carl. I jumped up every hour to touch her because she whimpered off and on all night. Once I felt her heartbeat beneath my hand, I crawled back into bed. It was dark. She was used to lights. It was quiet. She was used to rattling noises and whispering nurses.

During that long night, Lance got up with me several times and treated me like there was some emotions left between us. I wondered if Christina might still be the glue our ailing marriage needed.

By 6:30 in the morning, Christina was wet and hungry. I was delighted to begin my first real day of motherhood.

Living with Cystic Fibrosis began with baby steps. We were happy to learn that the CF Foundation was going to donate a mist tent for Christina's bed. When I'd met the president of the foundation, Eileen told me she had a CF child several years earlier and she had lived only a few years. At the time, I remember thinking, not me. That won't happen to Christina. They know more about CF now. The woman had been very kind and had promised to get everything we needed.

When she called us that morning, she said, "The foundation can afford the mist tent for you. Unfortunately, there's no money to buy the Propylene Glycol for the tent's mist or the Tobramycin she needs to inhale from the nebulizer before her postural drainage. But, I think that could change by July after the annual fund raiser."

"Wonderful news." I was light-headed with the information, especially now. Lance had been laid off again. I kept the news to myself. I tried to tamp down my fears. I was tired of being afraid. Had I made a mistake coming back to Salem? I'd already researched Multnomah County's Aid to Dependent Children program. It was just another name for welfare, which held such a stigma for me that I winced. But now Lance wasn't working. I knew I might not have a choice. My mind thrashed around for solutions.

Twelve days after we brought Christina home, Lance found another job. That was the good news. The bad news was that I must drive without him to Portland to pick up the mist tent from Abbey Rents. Our car was undependable, but I drove us to Portland with her small elevated seat, braced against bags on the car's passenger side floorboard. I cringe when I think of it now. In those days, we thought our children were safe before the advent of solid car seats. She could see me from the floor and I sang to her along with the music from the radio. She grinned and kicked her feet at me until she drifted to sleep. I was lucky that she was a good baby.

Mom went to Abbey Rents with me and the service consultant showed us how to measure and fill the chamber with Propylene Glycol and generally how to fit the frame and the mist tent over her crib.

"It is very important to clean it with vinegar every three or four days. It will stink, but once the meds run through it again, it will be fine. If you don't clean it, the mist can allow bacteria to build up and your baby will inhale that and…"

I felt my throat tighten up as I studied the instruction booklet. When I looked up at the man, he said, "It sounds overwhelming, but once you get going and it becomes a habit, you'll be surprised how fast you figure it out. Do you have your baby's medicine yet?"

"No, we are going to OHSU for prescriptions now."

After I thanked him and we had Christina and the apparatus stuffed into the car, we drove up the forested area to the medical clinic. My stomach tightened and then poof --- relief flooded through me. I knew this was just one more step to taking care of this child. Once we had the gallon of syrupy, clear Propylene Glycol and a bag filled with medicines and vitamins, we drove back to Mom's and put Christina to sleep. When she woke up, I planned to clap her, feed her and then drive back home again.

That afternoon, I called Lance and he suggested I spend the night because he didn't want me to drive home with the baby in the dark. It worked perfectly for me because I did not want to go home yet anyway.

My brothers picked up her Nutramagen milk from a nearby pharmacy and a few gallons of distilled water that were needed for the mist tent mixture. Dad helped us set up the metal frame. We dropped the mist tent cover over it and filled the chamber with the medicine and distilled water. And then we started the mist tent for the first time.

"Christina can't sleep in that haze. You can barely see her in there. It looks like a misty storm and she's coughing." Dad didn't like it much.

"She's supposed to cough, Dad. It clears her lungs of that thick mucus, remember?"

"But when she coughs, won't she choke? How do you know…?"

"Dad. She's on her belly. She's going to sleep. Don't make me crazy when I'm just getting around to figuring this stuff out."

He took a big breath and gave me a wan smile.

Mom closed the door to the den after putting in a night light. The baby was finally getting used to the dark, but not pitch blackness. She looked very tired. I felt exhausted too, but I took advantage of Mom during those days and weeks. The more she revved herself into super woman, the more I kept expecting it.

That morning, Christina woke about seven. Mom told me to go back to sleep for a while so she could have the baby to herself. I gladly agreed. Since Christina needed postural drainage three times a day and we now had the Tobramycin for her nebulizer to inhale, it was time to begin. Mom had been studying the process and when I got up, she was clapping Christina. With her legs stretched out in front of her, she had Christina laying on them with her small head pointed downward. Tap, tap, tap… In various positions, she clapped her first on the bottom of her lungs while she lay on her side and then on her back while she lay on her belly.

I squatted down beside her and stared into my baby's face. Her blue eyes stared back and then she grinned at me. She puffed out a tiny cough but nothing close to coughing up mucus. I guess we were just supposed to try until the little girl knew what to do.

Dr. Grach had instructed me to empty two capsules of enzymes into baby food fruit. Putting it into her milk bottle thickened it like oatmeal. The eye dropper was out of the question. So, I emptied the capsules into Christina's rice cereal and fruit. I soon learned the enzymes digested some fruits before I could get the spoon to her mouth. Bananas and pears turned into liquid immediately, so we changed to applesauce. That worked well and that little girl never tired of eating apple sauce. In fact, she loved it. That was an added bonus, of course.

Christina wheezed in her chest when she inhaled and exhaled through the mucus that stuck to her small lungs. I tried to get used to it, although it was frightening because I was unsure whether it was normal or if I should be worried about it. She took it in her baby stride.

When I clapped her later, her small face turned red when she coughed, but she could not expel any mucus.   And her poop smelled foul. I had been warned to expect it; the pancreatic granules were the culprit. I still had so much to learn.

Later, my friend Tina, walked in the door. "Let me come home with you," she said.   She was like a sister to me and had just begun her first year of nursing.   She was already in love with Christina and had bamboozled the NICU nursing staff to let her slip in to the unit many times during Christina's month at OHSU.

"Well, learning about CF might be good for you, auntie..."

"I can hold Christina's little seat between my feet on the floor."

"Perfect. Everything feels like happy sunshine. I will be glad to have you with us. I'm always nervous to take her in that spindly little car seat even though I brace it with blankets and the diaper bag." Driving the fifty miles from Portland to Salem was always easier if someone was with me because I constantly worried about being caught in traffic or having an accident with her little chair sitting helplessly on the floorboard.

To answer, Tina rubbed a finger along Christina's jaw line and made cooing noises.

A couple hours later, when we walked into our apartment, Lance scowled when he saw Tina. "What took you so long? I need dinner," he said, with a cigarette balanced between his lips. "I worked all day. I thought you would be here when I got home." Smoke swirled about the couch where he slouched.

When I placed Christina's baby chair down on the floor near him. He promptly lifted her out of the seat and poised her above his head as he squinted his eyes against the smoke from the cigarette pinched between his lips.

When I saw gusts of smoke float into Christina's face, I pulled Christina from his arms and watched him scowl.

"What the hell?"

"Don't blow smoke in her face, Lance. Dr. Grach told us how hard it is for her to breathe. You make it so much worse."

Lance yanked his cigarette from his mouth and stabbed the butt into the ashtray. "I'm hungry. Give her to me now, I'll hold her while you make us something to eat." As I walked away, still irritated, he followed with, "Oh, and bring me a beer, huh?"

Embarrassed, I glanced at Tina. I didn't want to fight with him, especially when she was there. I gritted my teeth and opened the fridge.

She rolled her eyes before pulling dishes and silverware out of the cupboard. I was too angry to think about food, but she rubbed circles over my back and whispered, "It's okay. I'll help." By the time her parents arrived the next day to take her home, I knew she was ready to go.

CHAPTER ELEVEN

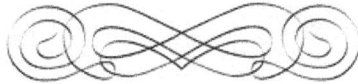

During those first few weeks, I gave myself pep talks about all the reasons that Lance acted the way he did. He hid his lack of confidence behind angry outbursts. And then he drank beer to live with it.

As April drew to an end, I was amazed at how content I felt. Christina was a joy. Each night after I clapped her, she snuggled into my arms to catch her breath and then I rocked her until her eyes started to close before I put her in the crib. With a pacifier, of course. It seemed the only thing that appeased her.

I wasn't ready to think about the future and whether it might still include Lance. Right then, I felt I had all I could manage with learning how to clap, feed, medicate and maintain Christina's health. I didn't intend to waste another minute looking through the rear-view mirror.

By the end of that first month at home, Christina's wheezing became more pronounced. The mist tent left her soaking wet each morning. Was that making her sick? Maybe I should take her off of it until her congestion lightened up? I was a nervous wreck. Could I do this? Christina coughed off and on all night. I turned off the mist tent, but I felt guilty.

Christina was really sick. When she coughed, her face turned a little bit blue. I called Dr. Grach to get an urgent appointment but she was unavailable. I called my local pediatrician Dr. Sessions and took her in immediately. After looking at her x-rays, he told me her lungs looked okay, but to take her out of the mist tent for short periods, not all night.

Christina started to improve. I guessed that I was doing this mother-thing right after all. Thank God.

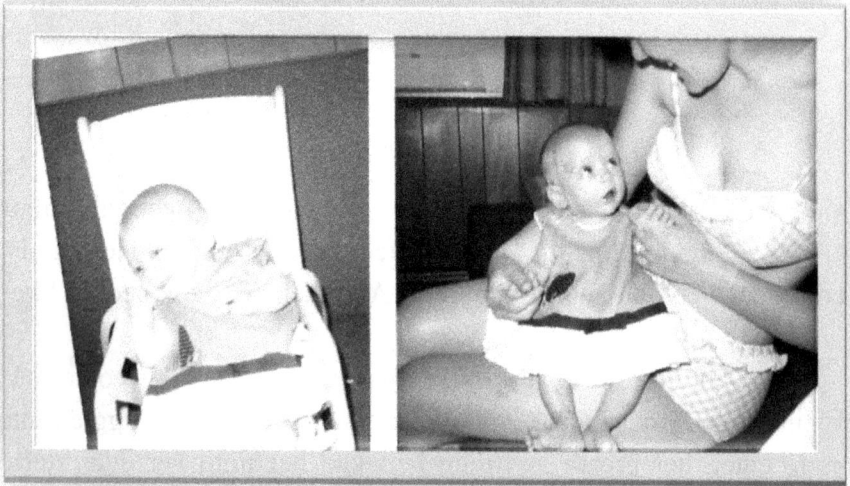

May 11, 1969 - My first Mother's Day.

It was a wonderful day. Christina's wheezing quieted, her coughing was minimal and her smiles made the day perfect. Mom brought most of the dinner. I made Jello. Our old neighbor/friends from Albany shared the day with us. Afterward, Christina was in such good spirits, Mom and Dad invited us to drive Bud and Caroline back home. Lance didn't want to go, so we girls tucked ourselves in between everyone.

It was just a few days afterward that Lance's grumpy behavior, temper and exhausting demands pushed me over the edge. If only I had enough money to move out. The rental cost of apartments was expensive. I knew I could move back to Mom and Dads, but I wanted to care for my baby on my own. I also knew I had endured his moodiness long enough.

It was time to become a single mother. I was sick of feeling unsettled while caring for Christina as I carried around a knot in my stomach. I gave in and drove to the county offices in Portland to apply for Aid to Dependent Children. I was approved to receive $125 per month. How could I rent an apartment, buy groceries and meet Christina needs? On the other hand, with Lance's disturbing personality and his sporadic employment, I knew I couldn't work outside the home. I had to either put up with his ways, worry about money with him or worry about money on my own. I was frantic.

When I returned home, he asked why dinner wasn't on the table. Of course, he did not know I had been gone at all. His attitude made my decision easier. Christina was happy when I handed him the nebulizer so she could inhale her medicine while I made dinner. She laughed and cooed, coughed, smiled and wheezed.

He was calmer after dinner. His usual demands were limited. He gave me a smile here and a hug. In fact, Lance wanted to clap Christina after he rewound the long tubing on the nebulizer machine. Something was off with him. Did I like it better when he was a jerk? No, but…could Christina and I survive on that small monthly stipend under the county's system? No to that too.

After I put her to bed, I sighed heavily and returned to the living room. My head was full of the meeting I'd had earlier that day. I flopped into a chair in the living room and turned to look at Lance.

He had an anxious look on his face. After he lit a cigarette and blew the smoke toward the ceiling, he said quietly, "Life is too difficult for me. I want a divorce because I'm in love with Shelley."

I was stunned to hear words that I had only guessed were true. The huge elephant in the room came roaring out of its box to face us at last. I put both hands to my head and felt my chest tighten. Before I could stop the words from charging back at him, I said, "That's too bad. You're a father now and that little baby needs you. I can't raise her alone." I guess I'd made my decision. Out of anger? Hurt? Exhaustion?

Cursing, he turned and stomped out.

My stomach didn't settle down until the door closed behind him. I took a deep breath. My hands were shaking, but damn, it felt good. In fact, I felt better than I'd felt in a long time. I had stood up to him.

Tina wanted to spend the weekend with us. Mom and her parents drove her to Salem, but Dad couldn't be civil to Lance, so he stayed home. Despite Lance's crankiness and my stress, Tina's presence soothed the edge off our troubles. Tina was sweet with Christina. I knew it was unfair to put her in the middle of the mess, but she was like a sister to me and she stood her ground. Within a few minutes, I knew Mom and her parents wanted to return to their own peaceful homes. Tina knew I was frustrated and angry, but frightened too.

As Tina was waiting for her parents to pick her up the next day, Lance stunned me all over again. "I want us to work on our marriage. Christina will be too mixed up if we break up and I do love you." (Again?).

Tina rolled her eyes.

After she left, I said, "Are you serious?" I found strength to stand up to him again. "If you want to save our marriage, we need to leave Salem, move away from Shelley. You are driving me crazy."

"Okay. I'll look for a house to rent in Turner." The small town was about twenty minutes south of Salem, closer to where he filled up his chip truck from the mill.

"Moving away can't arrive fast enough for me." I let him hug me and wondered if maybe this time he meant it?

Christina's monthly CF Clinic appointment in Portland was the end of May and I was anxious to talk with the doctor about her x-ray results. Her wheezing was persistent, but she wasn't cranky. The appointments tired her and parking places were limited. That day, I parked at the bottom of the hill and pushed her stroller all the way up to the clinic. I was so hot and sweaty by the time I arrived that I needed a shower. She, however, was delighted with the flowers along the way. She was more alert each day and I watched her for smiles or touched her soft cheek so her eyes would turn my way. My little girl now drank 2% milk; we hoped she would respond well, so we could stop the expensive Nutramigen formula. She was exhausted from being poked, prodded and x-rayed and I was dragging by the time we got to Mom's afterward, but that little imp was still smiling.

By Lance's first Father's Day, he still hadn't found a place to rent in Turner. He seemed anxious about our relationship and I was cautiously hopeful. When he was in the mood to be a nice guy, he could be fun, but otherwise, he wasn't. We drove to Portland to celebrate the special day. I'd sewed Dad a paisley vest and a cotton shirt for Lance. Mom had a big dinner planned. We played pinochle until early afternoon and then prepared spare ribs and Chinese rice. I made a pineapple upside down cake and we ate about 4:00 after Mel and Ellen, Tina's parents, arrived to share it with us.

Lance and I became Meg's daughter Ilsa's godparents at the Greek Orthodox Church baptismal ceremony. Christina and Ilsa are nine days apart and I imagined them growing up together like cousins.

Christina thrived during this period, but my relief was short lived. Lance had a major cold and I was worried sick that Christina would catch it. I tried to keep them away from each other, but he insisted on holding her. It was hot and stuffy in the duplex, so I opened all the windows even though I was afraid of bacteria or a virus floating in on the breeze.

I washed my hands raw to keep them clean around the baby. But within days, Christina caught Lance's cold. Her small body erupted in coughing and I was wild with worry. I clapped her and then let her nap inside the misting tent.

Lance said, "She could have caught that cold anywhere. I was careful." His eyes challenged me to argue.

What a goofy guy he was. I called the doctor and he told me to keep her in the mist tent, use the nebulizer, clap her as usual and keep the aspirator handy to clean out her nasal passages. He said she was clogged up with the thick mucus in her lungs. I knew that already.

Christina's wheezing got worse and I was very worried. I called Doernbecker Hospital in Portland. "Can I bring her up? I have faith in the doctors there," I cried.

When I told the nurse what I was doing for her, she said, "You are doing everything right."

"But Christina is fretful and sleeping more than usual."

"Let me check with the intake office and call you back."

Doernbecker called me the next day. I refused to call Shelley again. Twenty minutes would be all right, I told myself.

"Linda, I need you. Chrissy's cold is bad…real bad…pneumonia. Dr. Sessions says we need to get her to Portland. The car's out of gas. Lance is at work…and…"

"We're coming. Be ready," Linda's voice was fearful.

I paced the floor with Chrissy held tightly to my breast. I sang songs, "When I was just a little girl, I asked my mother… what will I be…?" then I continued with, "You are my sunshine, my only sunshine…" The songs came out in pieces as my throat clogged. I scratched out a quick note for Lance and then Linda and Stan roared into the driveway less than fifteen minutes later.

I ran to the car, jumped in with the diaper bag slapping against my hip and Stan headed north. We were all grim-faced. I knew Linda was afraid of reliving her own loss and Stan was too.

Chrissy kept coughing and crying as I rocked her back and forth. Please God, I screamed in my head, as I kept humming the songs over and over again. I kept swallowing the lump in my throat as Chrissy's cough filled the tense atmosphere in the car. I saw Stan grab at Linda's hand and they looked at each other. I knew we were all thinking the same thing. Don't let it happen… The words kept hammering inside my head…Oh

God. Not my baby…not yet please. I'm not ready to let her go. I fought tears and tried to keep my chin firm as Stan braked to a stop at the front door of the hospital. Linda and I rushed up the steps with Chrissy tightly swaddled in my arms. She was coughing, coughing, coughing.

Her cold had developed into pneumonia and they admitted her to feed her antibiotics. I smoothed the blonde hair off her forehead, wiped the sweat that ran in rivulets down her face as her coughing increased. I heard music and recognized Glen Campbell singing Wichita Lineman.

White coats pushed open the door and Chrissy's little body was taken from me by two doctors, one friendlier than the other.

And then we waited.

When the friendlier doctor found us pacing in the waiting room, he pulled me aside. "I'm sorry it's taking so long. But we have to run more tests to find out why she's taken such a dive the last two days."

"Two days without the mist tent? Could that have done it? She was so wet and…"

He shook his head. "I doubt it. I'll be back when I can."

Linda and Stan wanted to get me food, coffee, anything.

"All I want is Chrissy…nothing else…" I was ravaged.

Suddenly the doctor returned. "I suggest you go home," he said kindly. "We will be keeping her for a while. She's in very good hands. We have to stabilize her breathing and change the antibiotic. We can't do anything until we see the test results tomorrow."

"Can I stay in her room over night?"

"No, please go home and come back in the morning."

I found a telephone. "Mom?" I began to cry so I handed the phone to Linda.

"I'm coming, Linda. God, this is too much, isn't it?" Mom fought tears too, but didn't allow herself to pass on her fears to either of us.

I looked at Stan as he stood behind Linda with his hands gripping her shoulders. He stood over six feet tall and his gentle eyes made people relax around him. "It will be okay," he said and then he winked at me.

His smile wrapped around us like a big hug. And now he will soon be a Daddy again, I thought. Linda will be given a second chance…just six months for them to wait. I prayed that their baby would not have CF.

"Here we go again, honey," Mom said as she hugged me the minute she walked through the door. "Don't worry. They'll take good care of her. Have faith. You did it before…"

"We will be going now," Linda said and they walked out hand in hand, each too afraid to talk about what might be in store for them with their second chance at parenthood.

I let Mom take me home.

"Lance called, honey."

"What did he say?"

"Just that he wants you to call him. He'll try to come up tomorrow…" she finished lamely.

I stared at her.

The next morning, Lance drove to Portland. Neither of us had slept much. By two, we were told that my poor baby was still coughing, coughing, coughing. She could barely catch her breath before the next batch of coughing erupted again. I kept the faith, believing that the doctors could resolve her terrible discomfort. And I vowed that the next cold Lance got would mean hands off as far as Christina was concerned. If he argued with me, I would grab her and leave.

We spent the night in Portland. When I called the hospital the next morning, I was relieved to hear Christina spent a fairly good night. Relief swamped me. By the time we arrived at her bedside, her eyes smiled a wee bit…enough to give us hope. She was more alert than she had been in the past few days and her eyes followed the nurse as she attended to her. They told us that Christina was holding her own and I should stay home. Christina needed rest. The idea of not going up immediately didn't sit well with me, but Lance, Mom and Dad agreed, so we bought some fried chicken and packed it with the cake I baked last night to keep myself busy.

We drove to Timothy Lake near Mt. Hood and ate our picnic lunch. I was too wired to enjoy myself, so we stayed only an hour. And then on the way home, the men wanted to stop in the small town of Zig Zag for a beer.

My mind screamed, *no, I want to see my baby.*

Later that evening, we returned to the hospital and the four of us were delighted to see the difference in Christina. Lance lost his doldrums when she smiled at him. I hoped the scare would make him more cautious in the future when he was sick. He seemed to be distancing himself from her again. Was it because her illness reminded him of his dead sister and brother?

My tiny girl had an IV tube taped to her head. I stumbled when I saw her but she seemed unaware that it was attached into her little body. I remember praying that the antibiotics would kill the pneumonia and the oxygen would help her breathe better.

The doctors were arguing about a procedure she needed. One doctor argued the loudest. He wanted to place a microscopic tube down her throat to fill air into her deflated lung. The other doctors said it could kill her, but Dr. Brooks said without the procedure she would die anyway. Dr. Grach was against it also. I watched all the doctors inside the glass-enclosed room. They shook their hands angrily to make their points.

My mind turned numb and I went into the corner away from everyone. All of the research matter had not prepared me for the utter hopelessness that I felt that day and I pressed my hands to my eyes to stop the torrent of tears that wanted to escape.

A man's voice startled me. "I'm Dr. Brooks. I didn't get a chance to introduce myself yesterday in the middle of all the chaos. We are all concerned about this little one. We can't decide whether her distress is caused from mucus plugs in her tiny lungs or the bacterial infection. We changed antibiotics and she has shown some slight signs of relief. We are studying her x-rays again."

I turned and he joined a group of other doctors in the glass-conference room. Dr. Grach saw me and we nodded to each other. She looked sad and worried. I watched the meeting with growing curiosity as Dr. Brooks shook his head and seemed to be arguing with the others. All I could think about was Dr. Grach looking sad and worried.

"What do you think is going on in there?"

"I don't know, Mom." My mind galloped at top speed as thoughts raced through my head. Don't do this, God. Don't take her away from us. If you're there…please don't do it. I didn't realize I was holding my breath until Dr. Brooks was beside me again. I exhaled jerkily when I saw his forbidding look.

"Is your husband here?" He looked around us.

"No, he and my Dad went for coffee."

"Well, we need you in the conference room."

I followed him into the glass enclosure. My heart hammered against my rib cage and I wondered how I could walk without breathing. There were seven people inside. Men and women, all dressed in starched white clothing. I felt weak and someone pushed me into a chair. Mom waited outside. The group sat in a circle. I knew it was a training hospital and I should have been used to it, but why did I feel so scared this time? I looked from one face to the other.

Dr. Brooks began, "One of Christina's lungs is collapsed."

My breath caught. "What…?"

"I want to expand it immediately," he said as he stared at me.

I froze as if I'd turned to stone. I knew I couldn't lose this beautiful child now. I couldn't. "Yes, please do it," I cried. Then I noticed the grim faces around me. "If it will save my baby, what's the matter?" I was scarcely breathing.

Mom must have seen the conflicting emotions flitting across my face through the glass. I saw her fingers dig into the sides of the vinyl chair outside the room.

"The only time a direct laryngoscopy has been used," he explained, "which means I would be placing a tube down the throat to suck mucus plugs from the trachea, has been on older patients with considerably larger throats."

"And the success ratio…" another doctor ventured.

"The success ratio is slim on a baby as tiny as your daughter." Dr. Brooks said the words as he looked directly into my eyes.

"We can't agree on whether we should expose Christina to this extreme technique," said Dr. Grach as she reached for my hand.

Dr. Brooks, I realized seemed to be standing alone in his beliefs to use the technique on Chrissy. What to do?

"She will die if her lung isn't re-inflated. So what is the problem? I mean, really…what is the problem?" he said urgently.

"Yes, what is the problem if that might save her life?" Nobody seemed to be listening to me because they were all studying each other.

Everyone began talking at once. I was afraid to make any more contributions. I will not cry, I thought. I WILL NOT. I tried to still the trembling of my body and force my mind into calmness. I raised my head and let them talk. When it comes to a decision, they will tell me. My heart thumped inside my chest as if a million heart beats ran rampant. And then I couldn't help myself. I said, "Dr. Brooks is right."

Everyone looked at me. The other doctors still looked dubious. And then Dr. Brooks' eyes blazed in triumph. He squeezed my shoulder. "We can prepare Christina right away then."

"Yes, I'm depending on you. She's in your hands…literally." I trusted his clear, gray eyes and the confidence that stared from behind them.

The room cleared. Everyone went their separate ways. Dr. Grach reached for my hand and led me over to my Mom.

Then I promptly burst into tears as Mom folded me in her arms.

"Tell me," Mom whispered, feeling shut out and numb.

"I'm so glad you're here, Mom…they're going to operate now." After I dried my tears, I sat in an ugly green chair near Chrissy's steel-framed crib. I told her in a rush of words about the meeting. "I know if

Christina has a chance I have to trust him. He's so sure the suction tube will save her. We have to do whatever we can…don't we? She's still so tiny, Mom. This operation is usually on adults, but this time…"

Dr. Brooks entered the room as Christina started coughing harshly again. He turned toward me and clasped my hand and said just two words, "Trust me." And then he was gone.

I walked over to my baby's crib. I stared at the monitors and traced the electronic fragility of her life. I could barely see her body beneath the mist. Her CF regimen didn't stop…her coughing didn't stop… I slumped against the bed while Mom caressed my back. The waiting began again.

"Lance should be here," Mom muttered.

"I know, Mom. He'll be walking around the corner any time." I thought of Lance then and thought why now? Why does he want to move us to Turner now? It's not that far from Salem and Shelley, but why now? To begin again, he said. How many AGAINS would we have? I thought of our last conversation before Christina got so sick. He said, "I'll be who you want me to be, away from Shelley." What timing, I thought…with Christina here…but maybe he's right.

"Hey, princess," Dad said as he spun me around for a hug. It felt good. I pretended I was a little girl again. Lance stood outside the door.

"We'll be taking Christina now," a nurse said as she grabbed the end of the crib. She pushed it out of the room and next to the nurse's station. My eyes closed as I whispered a prayer. Dad stroked Mom's arms and pulled us into a group hug.

I moved to Christina's side and reached inside to touch her soft baby hand. Minutes ticked by before they actually moved her again. Her little fist had managed to curl around my finger in a gentle grip as she labored with her loud, honking breaths. She stared at me with eyes that seemed to say, "Why, Mommy?" I pulled her hand toward me and placed a tender kiss on her fingers and smiled as the nurses pushed her away.

"Let's sit down," Mom persuaded.

Please, Lord. Don't let this be the last time I see this baby alive.

Mom whispered to Dad, "She has been pale and dusky looking. Her coughing has been a never ending circle of crying, coughing, crying, coughing…then she would lay quiet and exhausted until it started all over again."

Lance stood and stared out the window away from us.

Within the hour, Christina was returned. "We will do it twice more within the next twenty four hours, so don't give up because her coughing is still intense," Dr. Brooks promised.

Back at Mom's afterward, I wanted to put my feet up, lean my head against her favorite chair and rest. Was Dr. Brooks right? My mind was a hurricane. I wanted quiet, but Lance had other ideas.

"Let's go listen to country music somewhere."

I groaned, but Dad thought it might get our mind off of Christina's woes. We found a place on the Columbia River, where Lance drank beer, smoked a few cigarettes, fully content to remain even though the music blared and we couldn't talk. We pulled him away at midnight.

Since he worked the next day, we visited Christina on our way home. Her face was wreathed in smiles when she saw us. Her coughing was still horrible, but the nurses said they were encouraged. Her baby smiles told me that also. However, I'm sure I had skid marks on the floor where Lance pulled me from her bedside.

Mom called me from the hospital that afternoon with good news. The oxygen continued with mist and medicines, but the antibiotic line had been removed from her head. The nurse woke her up so Mom could hold her. She was smiling. I was hopeful.

"Christina's lung is now inflated." Dr. Brooks's voice sounded excited as he continued, "This is the first time we've used it on an infant and now that we know it works, it will save others. Thank you for having confidence in me." I could hear the smile in his voice as the tears rolled down my face. Antibiotics stopped on the fifth hospital day when she continued to show improvement. She smiled, coughed less and her skin turned pink again. I was so relieved that Dr. Brooks fought for the procedure. Every time we saw each other in the corridors of the hospital, we would share a special smile. I thanked him repeatedly and he glowed in his success. Christina's song sang sweet for him too because he knew she'd paved the way to help other infants.

Lance rented us a duplex in Turner. He was full of positive news and we hoped to move in for Christina's homecoming. Everything he told me sounded rosy and I believed him. I told him I would return to Salem and begin packing.

"Once Christina's vitals stabilize and she doesn't require oxygen or show pneumonia, she will be yours to take home again." Dr. Brooks' face gleamed with satisfaction.

"Thank you so much." My stomach was doing cartwheels.

"Christina might be released as soon as tomorrow."

When I heard the doctor's words, I was happy, but frightened. I struggled with the idea of bringing her home, still living beside Shelley in Salem. I didn't want to watch the woman come and go or wonder…He appeared committed to our marriage now but who knew?

Christina was released two days later. Linda and I raced to Portland, grabbed her before they could change their mind and drove to Mom's house. More photos. More hugs. Christina looked and acted healthy again. A few coughs, but nothing like last week. I nebulized her, clapped her and then we headed back to Salem. I hoped the duplex in Turner would soon give us a new start.

But it was not to be.

CHAPTER TWELVE

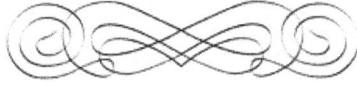

Nine days later, my world fell apart again. Would I never learn? Lance was still seeing Shelley. I confronted him and he admitted it. I packed up the baby with everything I could fit into my car and drove to Portland. I told Mom and Dad I'd left Lance and they did not question me. I said I would take my chances on surviving with the monthly $125 stipend from the county.

Mom and Dad were understanding even though my life had been a yo-yo of emotions and bad decisions for the past year. What would I do without them, I wondered? What do young, single mothers do when they have nobody to lean on? Is that when they give a baby up for adoption? The thoughts ran rampant through my head as I hugged my child, heard her wispy wheeze and felt her arms curl around my neck.

The first day away from my marriage was another first. July 20, 1969, American spacemen Neil Armstrong and Buzz Aldrin landed on the moon. We took photos off the television screen. I cut out the newspaper article to save in my treasure box. It was amazing, a day I will not forget.

I felt more relaxed than I had in months. I pulled weeds and trimmed plants with Mom in her yard. The physical energy soothed my mind. Tina brought over all the makings for a fabulous dinner afterward. Fried chicken, baked beans, fresh biscuits and potato salad. Meg brought Ilsa over and everyone watched our astronauts walk on the moon and shove the American flag in the moon's soil.

CF Clinic day was long and tiring but the news was good. Dr. Grach told me she was glad Dr. Brooks did the procedure because it saved Christina's life, but she had been afraid to agree with his decision. Christina's lungs were clear, the enzymes were working in applesauce and I now felt like a professional therapist. She cried when the nurse gave her the baby shots, but she fell asleep on the way back to Moms.

Dr. Grach surprised me when she said, "Living in Portland will be good for Christina. I am astonished that you stayed with Lance as long as you did, but it will be a hard job alone."

When I got home, Dad took Christina for a stroller ride after her nap. I heard him whistle all the way down the street. It was warm outside and the fresh air surely did her some good.

Neva, my mother-in-law, called. Her voice was filled with disappointment when she said, "I'm sorry that Lance is chasing Shelley again. I am worried about you and Christina, but I am glad you are with Neyda and Koffee." I didn't have answers or reassurances except to tell her I would bring Christina to visit when I could.

I often made dinner and cleaned up the kitchen; I wanted to hold up my end of the bargain in exchange for their giving us a roof over our heads, food and loving support.

The weather turned hot. Christina had a heat rash something fierce and her breathing became rugged, but between me and Mom, we kept her cool, clapped and happy. I returned to the county offices to accept the county money; I would receive my first check along with several books of food stamps. I sighed over that one and tried to ignore the stigma of welfare. Luckily, the CF Foundation was able to fund her medicine. I was sick to think that burden would be on my Mom and Dad.

When I asked Mel and Ellen Berger for a short-term loan to rent an apartment that I had found nearby, they wrote a check without a hint of hesitation. I felt blessed. What did young women do when they had nobody to lean on?

Our apartment was on the upper floor of a turn-of-the-century house. A place of my own. I was dizzy with relief, filled with fear, uncertain about life, but I ecstatically embraced single motherhood.

Lance had been silent since I left Salem.

Moving day. Mom and Ellen helped me pack up the duplex. We were in and out so fast, I could hardly call it home. The women moved like cyclones, threw things in the car and filled boxes fast.

Lance was there as we packed up everything. "I don't want you to leave me." He began to cry and tried to hug me. "I changed my mind. I didn't mean it."

I stared at him. "I am leaving. Period."

And I did.

The next day, I left Christina with Ellen in Portland. Mom and I led my posse, consisting of Dad, Mel Berger and his son, Ken, who hauled a large U-Haul trailer to carry the furniture and boxes. When we arrived at my new Portland apartment, my brother Steven and his friends helped us unload everything. Up and down the stairs. I loved it. Old wood, newly-painted walls, tiny kitchen, two bedrooms and a claw-foot tub. I could hardly wait until we could sleep there. It was a new beginning.

Delicious peace. Sleeping in my new apartment, Christina and I each had our own bedrooms. Silence was golden. The next few days were busy as I unpacked in between clapping Christina and giving her medicines. She thrived in our new home and so did I. When Mom and Dad invited me out to dinner, I called Tina to babysit. I'm not sure who was more thrilled; me to go out to dinner or Tina to have Christina all to herself.

It was a quiet Sunday when I prepared me and Christina for a day trip south to Albany so paternal grandparents could see her. And Lance. I wasn't thrilled, but it was fair. The day was nice and even though I was nervous about seeing him, he was too happy to see Christina to be nasty.

Yes, I was now on welfare. I looked at the $125 check. The books of food stamps were in the envelope. I was humbled. My apartment did not have a washer or dryer, so the plan was I would wash our laundry at Mom's house. Another blessing. So many diapers.

The days blended into one another. Christina and I ate at Mom and Dads or they came to our place, sometimes bringing the meal with them. Mom bought me a stroller so I could walk around the city, especially back and forth to hers or Ellen's houses. Sometimes, Mom finished our laundry. We worked out a plan to help stretch my monthly check; food stamps could only be used for food. I bought Mom and Dad food in exchange for cash so I could buy the staples I needed such as soap, shampoo, cleaning supplies. What did people like me do without loving parents?

Mom bought Christina a motorized swing. I am unsure who enjoyed it more; Christina or Mom? Their grins mirrored each other. Winding the spring-loaded handle was loud. And she loved it because she knew she would start moving and her feet kicked with excitement.

One of the many blessings of living in Portland again was that I reconnected with my good friend, Meg. We loved sharing motherhood stories, our baby's antics and the many pleasures and pressures that came with motherhood. She and little Ilsa strolled over to see us or we went to see them. Ilsa is more of an extrovert than Christina, who is more shy and sensitive to loud noises, but they liked seeing each other.

By the third week of August, Christina was sick again. No matter how careful I was, the poor girl could not fight germs that lingered around her. I made an appointment with Dr. Grach. I hoped she was teething. It seems that every time she coughed too much or was cranky, my mind went to a dark place.

Was it CF or baby issues?

I was right. My girl was teething.

In September, Christina was six months old. Linda and Stan drove to Portland to take us home with them to Albany. We packed our suitcase, the mist tent, baby swing, playpen, food and medicines in a huge bag. It felt like I was moving again, even though it was only for four days. It was good to get away from the city and visit with good friends. Lance came to visit Christina. He was sweet as honey to me.

He spent all four days begging me to be his wife again. I was a mess. I was vulnerable. I was lonely. I was irrational. Seeing him with Christina made me feel guilty. He made promises, promises and more promises. After all I'd gone through moving away, leaning on my family and friends, could I really move back with him? Did he change that much?

Mom was livid and I didn't blame her. We spent hours talking about the situation. And then I made up my mind. As I write this part of my life, actually put it into words, my utter stupidity turns me numb. Mom couldn't get through to me because all I could think of was Lance's kisses and his promise that this time would be different.

Lance drove to Portland and met me at Moms. While I was out of the room, Mom told me he started to pick up Christina with a cigarette in his mouth. Smoke was swirling around their heads. She raised a hand and said, "Please put out your cigarette because the smoke clogs her lungs." He stared at her for a heartbeat, put his burning cigarette down in the ashtray next to his chair and lifted her to his shoulder.

She told me that she marched over, picked up his cigarette and stubbed it out. She was right but where was the line I needed to draw between my husband and mother? He had not put Christina's health first. If I'd been in the room, I would have done the same thing. He spent the weekend, his promises lingered and my hopes increased. I was blind to the misery that lay ahead. I had to hand it to Mom and Dad though; we shared meals and played cards and they bit their tongues. But I delayed moving. Not yet.

Mom had a photo coupon, so we took Chrissy to Emerson's Studio. I'd sewn a little black and white dress with a big white collar for the photo shoot. I couldn't take my eyes off of her. Adorable, of course. The photographer was quick and entertaining, but Chrissy could barely sit up alone. In a heartbeat, she'd placed her on the table with blankets stuffed around her and then, pop. Chrissy was on the floor. She was frightened more than hurt, so the smiles were slow. I think all the photos had tears on her cheeks but that imp still smiled for the camera.

Chrissy giggled, laughed, smiled at everyone and just generally entertained all of us. She was still small, delicate. Most days one could not tell she had CF at all. In fact, if I didn't use the nebulizer, clap her and put all the enzymes in her applesauce to digest her food, I could almost forget, except for her wheezing, of course.

She loved the independence of sitting in her walker; she was a demon on wheels. One day, I heard her clicking through our small apartment's living room while I stood in the even-smaller kitchen. I was backed up against the counter when she swung around the corner. I saw a racing gleam sparkle in her eyes. Before I could stop her, she'd pushed off with one foot and barreled toward me. I had to actually jump straight over her body to save myself. Her speed and agility amazed me. I knew she would probably have broken both my legs. How a tiny girl could maneuver that chair on wheels with such speed amazed me and still does as I visualize her careening around that corner.

My friend, Meg, picked up Chrissy's medicines from the OHSU pharmacy to save me the trip of driving and parking up on the hill. It was an arduous experience and since she worked there every day, it was a wonderful boon to have her there.

The Oregon rains had begun and the view from the windows became dreary. But it did not stop my Mom from visiting after her work day to pick up our laundry to take it home. There was just no way to thank this woman.

It still felt strange when my parents came over and I served coffee and dessert, just like I was a grownup. It was a treat to have them sit and chat so I could wait on them for a change.

Another CF Clinic day, but it was for my brother-in-law Roy, not for Chrissy. I had been trying to get him into the clinic since he had never been there. Mom drove me to the hospital so I could visit with Neva. Her grandmother heart needed to see Chrissy. Roy fought the clinicians and everything they told him. I imagine it was because it was new to him and he was a teenager. Neva was having a difficult time with him. I sensed her fears since she had already buried two children and one grandson from this devastating disease. He did not attend the CF Clinic afterward.

By October, Chrissy had another cold, which was beginning to be the never-ending story for her. This time, her continuous, choking cough and clogged nose made her gasp for breath and her eyes dripped. When she sucked on her bottle, the coughing started again. She had so much trouble breathing that her face turned blue. I called the doctor and they told me to bring her in immediately. After waiting for x-rays and blood tests, we were relieved to hear it was not pneumonia this time. The little girl had a rotten cold again. Every time she sucked on the nipple of her bottle, she coughed and could not catch her breath. I died a little each time her face turned blue. Her eyes went into panic mode in tandem with my heartbeats.

I had forgotten that Mom and Dad had lent Lance a credit card so he could buy gas to visit me and Christina. I assumed he had returned it weeks before and paid the bill. But, Mom received notice the end of October that the unpaid bill totaled $350. The credit card company was suing them. When Mom called Lance, he wasn't home.

Why did I trust this man? I made an appointment with the Legal Aid Society and started divorce proceedings. Chrissy's cold got worse. She coughed so hard that her body was weak and she just lay on my shoulder. My mother-in-law came to visit and between Neva and Mom, they sat with her while I sat in a chair across town telling my story to a divorce lawyer. My mind was in turmoil; I knew it was the right thing to do, but my heart was stripped to pieces.

The next day, Chrissy perked up and the coughing lessened as she gained strength and found her smile again. A few days later, Mom took me to the bank so we could open a savings account for Chrissy...I cashed in all my savings bonds to pay a portion of that damned gas card bill, and left $25 in her new account.

Lance apologized, paid some money toward the card, and then asked me to bring Chrissy to Albany for the weekend. He missed her and wanted to talk with me again. My stomach was wrenched from its moorings again, but I agreed. When he picked me and Chrissy up, we drove to Mom's to pick up our clean clothes.

She spoke to me, but she was too angry to speak to him. I felt her pain and knew she thought I'd lost my pride, but I had to figure out which way to go. Divorce or not to divorce? Live as a single parent as I'd hoped to during my pregnancy? Or admit failure because it was so hard doing it alone with Chrissy's disease looming over us every day? I guess I needed someone to lean on and Lance kept getting in my foggy way. That weekend, he had sweet talked me into returning to him, not just thinking about it. Mom didn't try to talk me out of my decision. Guess she'd just given up. But I was not leaving for a while. Not yet.

A few days later, Linda drove up from Albany about noon so Meg and I took her to the big Jantzen Sportswear fabric sale while Mom watched both the little girls. When we returned about five, the girls were both sleeping soundly.

Within minutes, Lance called. "I have been waiting over an hour for you at your apartment. Where are you?"

I asked Linda to follow us to the apartment, but Lance arrived at Mom's instead. Impatient and angry, he pulled up to the curb at the same time Dad drove into the driveway. When my Dad saw new magnesium wheels on Lance's pickup, he nearly had apoplexy because he still owed them money on the credit card for gas.

Chrissy needed distilled water for her mist tent the next morning. Mom called to offer, "Do you want me to babysit Chrissy so Lance can drive you up to the hospital to get it?"

Lance said, "I don't have enough gas. Can someone else drive you?"

Instead of my remembering how many times we went without distilled water, vitamins or heat in the apartment before I left him the last time, I focused on now. I am not making this story up. As I type it I am amazed that my mother still speaks to me. She must have thought I needed an IQ test. Vulnerable? Lonely? Stupid?

Before Thanksgiving, Lance drove up for the weekend and bravely talked with Dad about the gas bill. They walked over to the tavern to speak alone. Mom and I talked about everything again, watched Chrissy play and fall asleep before the men returned. I don't know what happened, but when they returned, they were friends again.

Mom and I spent the day making *Rosquettes*, our traditional Spanish cookies, for Christmas. As the scent of the wine-drenched cookies permeated through the air from the oven, my life almost felt normal again.

Chrissy was accepting her postural drainage therapy as normal. I was amazed that she ate her applesauce three times a day filled with grainy granules mixed into each little dish. And she nearly licked the bowl despite its stink.

Over the next few days, Lance coaxed himself back into my family. Hope flickered to life again that I could mesh my family back together.

As the astronauts splashed down in three parachutes after their thrilling ride to and from the moon, I packed for the move to our new duplex apartment to Turner. Our new home had a huge grassy back yard that led down to a creek. I knew Chrissy would love it. Lance and I packed all day after Thanksgiving while Mom kept Chrissy all night. She is a pro at caring for Chrissy with the nebulizer, clapping her and placing her into the mist tent to sleep. So many boxes; the packing was nearly finished.

Over the next few days, I thanked everyone for helping me pack up once again. My brothers have been so good and supportive. My parents? I shake my head remembering how they kept supporting me even though they were sure I was making a huge mistake. They hoped they were wrong…

I cleaned the duplex like a mad woman and we moved in. Christina loved looking out the low-slung windows and smiled constantly between her wretched coughing spasms. The mist tent covered her new crib and I prayed that our lives would finally be normal.

By my birthday on December 14th, the new duplex felt like a home at last. The rooms were spotless, Chrissy's room had a nice carpet and the crib seemed gigantic around her little body. She was nine months old and raced around the house at high speed in that little walker, grinning with her pacifier squeezed between her teeth.

By Christmas Eve, our life was good as we prepared for our traditional family Christmas Eve dinner at a local restaurant in Portland. When we arrived at Mom's, the family was ready. Chrissy was perfect, so perfect in fact that all her uncles and grandpa kept giving her little treats. By the end of the evening on our way out of the restaurant, she spewed those various treats all over me and the floor. Poor girl. She had happily crammed everything into her mouth. Once she vomited, everyone laughed but me.

Chrissy and I both had colds again. When that little girl started coughing like that, her face and neck turned blotchy red. Her body shook all over, so I held her to soothe her back to safety. Lance tried to help, but she only wanted Momma or grandma during those horrible episodes. Despite a lovely Christmas and while hope bloomed for us again, dread curled around my insides as I watched Chrissy fight for each breath.

By New Year's Eve, I knew something was terribly wrong. I hadn't felt good for the past week and thought my menstrual cycle was a hard one. Cramps began about 2:00 p.m. Hard cramps. Chrissy was asleep when they got worse and I ran to the bathroom.

Once I sat down, the cramps were so bad that I nearly missed the huge bundle of blood that fell into the toilet. Miscarriage. I heard Lance's chip truck barreling through town beside our duplex that took him to the truck filling area. I bundled a towel between my legs and rushed to the window and waved wildly at him, hoping he realized I needed him. He pulled the cable to honk his horn and raced by with a hand wave.

By the time he arrived home forty-five minutes later, I was still on the toilet. Thankfully, Chrissy was still asleep.

He was ragged with worry.

After a call to the doctor, my new neighbor Helen stayed with Chrissy while Lance drove me to the Salem Hospital. I remember laying on the back seat of the car wondering what happened. He kept asking me if I was okay over and over again. Of course I wasn't okay. I hadn't known I was pregnant. An hour or so later, as the doctor performed my D & C, he called my mother. And she came to the rescue again, agreeing to spend a few days caring for me and Chrissy. Now I not only owed my parents, my brothers and my friends. I owed Mom's boss for giving her the time off from work. I was beginning to wonder if I was ever going to become an adult and stand on my own two feet.

CHAPTER THIRTEEN

I refused to believe that my lost baby was a black omen as the new year began. In my heart, I knew that my body aborted that baby because he or she was not physically whole. It was my second miscarriage, after all. Instead, I focused on my little girl and strengthening my marriage. Determined, I took a deep breath and put the sadness of my loss behind me.

Again, my family and friends came to the rescue. Mom, Dad and Tina arrived to greet Linda. Their arms were filled with food. Weakened from loss of blood and the after pains from the D & C, I wasn't much help.

Chrissy thought it was a party and zipped around in her wheeled seat from person to person like a yo-yo. Mom and Tina both knew the regiment to fill the nebulizer, squeeze the rubber bulb to spray the medicine into her nostrils and clap her chest to make her cough. And if Mom cooked when Chrissy needed therapy, Tina took over.

Tina prepared her baby food.

I enjoyed the company.

Lance watched the New Year's Day football game and tried to stay out of everyone's way.

Dad drove back to Portland after dinner.

That night, our gas furnace blasted into the living room every time the temperature rolled down to 68. The sporadic noise kept Mom awake, so she lowered the thermostat to keep the thing quiet. We always left Chrissy's bedroom door open so the heat would slip into her room. With her door open, her whimpering during the night was another thing Mom wasn't used to. So, with the heat nearly off and the intermittent snuffling sounds coming out of her room, Mom didn't sleep much. And we were chilled by morning because the heater didn't pop on during the night. In January, that was a long and very cold sleep.

The after pains continued through the night and every time I stood up, I felt faint. Mom and Tina shooed me to the couch while they cared for Chrissy during the day and washed our laundry at the laundromat. Thankfully, the neighbor next door offered us the use of her dryer. She was very kind to me and fell in love with my baby. She baked and delivered a frosted cake to our back door and then she popped out again.

When Dad arrived after work, we enjoyed the steaming pot of chicken and dumplings Mom made for us. Chrissy slurped the gravy as if it was ambrosia. I think Dad arrived to see Chrissy and we were a trip bonus. He slept on the floor of her bedroom in a sleeping bag and we left the gas furnace on that night, regardless of its blasting, noisy gusts.

And it's a good thing Mom didn't tamper with it. We got up to snow on the ground. The two large living-room windows had a view of north and west. The huge snowflakes sprinkled down on the world in slow motion, shimmery and pristine. Chrissy's large, blue eyes gleamed as she stared out the window from her walker. Turning her eyes toward me, she pointed out the window as if to tell me what was happening out there. She moved her walker from one corner of the window to the next, grinning and craning her neck to peek around the corner, probably wondering where the white stuff was coming from.

Mom and Tina braved the weather to drive thirty minutes away into Salem to purchase groceries. I worried about them driving in the snow, but they returned a couple hours later well laden with food. They prepared a week's worth of meals for Chrissy, took our laundry to the laundromat again, cleaned up the house, made lunch and put Chrissy to bed after clapping her again. I'm sure by the time Mom, Dad and Tina left that night, they were too exhausted to talk on the road home.

By the end of that day, I felt like myself again, but I nearly cried as I watched them drive away. Chrissy wanted to go home with them too. She either felt my vibes or she'd been hugged so much the past few days, she didn't want it to stop. She'd loved being the star in front of Mom's video camera.

The next few days rained ice and Lance couldn't drive the chip truck, so he entertained Chrissy while I caught up on housework, finished unpacking odd boxes and prepared Chrissy's food. The cold seemed to permeate the rooms despite the furnace blowing heat into the house. I worried about Chrissy and kept the poor girl so bundled up, she could hardly move her arms in the layers of clothing I had on her.

Chrissy thrived as 1970 beckoned us through the New Year's window. She changed daily, more adorable than the day before; I knew I was prejudiced, but with her reddish gold hair, lovely bright-blue eyes and that one dimple, who could argue?

The days passed without much adversity and for that I was grateful. Chrissy's coughing was minimal and she wasn't sniffling. I hung a blanket over both the big windows to keep the heat inside the apartment. She thought I was playing a game. Every time I turned around, her little fingers yanked at the corners to see what I was hiding behind the curtain.

She was small, but fast, as I said before. The duplex was not large and you'd think a little person would be easy to keep track of, but she still managed to yank the blanket down on top of her when I wasn't looking. When I heard her screaming from the living room, I raced in there and started laughing because the blanket covered her like a tent. Her hands scrambled around like a bird caught in a net. Quickly removing it, I picked her up, felt her arms whip around me and I soothed her to silence.

I'd hoped we could drive up to Portland that Sunday, but Lance was too sick from a hangover, so we decided to stay home. His beer drinking had escalated over the past weeks and I didn't like it. We also couldn't afford to buy so much beer. I told myself that the struggle and responsibility of a sick child was working overtime on his nerves. I'm glad I didn't drink much; we didn't have enough money to scrape together for anything extra. But he just didn't get it. Thank goodness I didn't smoke cigarettes. One in the family with that habit was expensive enough.

It was during those times in our lives that I wished I could get a job so I could control our money situation. But, of course, with Chrissy's needs it was impossible. It took three hours each day to nebulize and clap her to knock the phlegm loose from her lungs. Another couple of hours to prepare her food and just be a mother. And we didn't have a washer and dryer. I knew lots of young people did not have those luxuries, but taking our laundry to the laundromat with a baby, especially one with Cystic Fibrosis, was a major event.

One day while I was at the local laundromat, I was waiting for the washer to finish. There was a café attached to the washroom, so I sat down with Chrissy and nursed my coffee. I pushed Chrissy's stroller back and forth with my foot and made faces at her to get her to smile. Country music thrummed from the sound system, and Chrissy had been fretting because she disliked loud noises. That day, the music was louder than usual, but I couldn't leave the washer alone to walk her up and down the sidewalk while I waited because it was too cold.

An older man and woman sat in the booth next to me and ordered an early lunch, while watching me coax Chrissy to smiles again. I knew they had been paying attention to her because they said hello and the man kept smiling at her. He nodded toward me when I caught his eye.

The woman's lips tightened and said, "What kind of a mother are you to take a sick baby outside in this cold?" Her eyes were angry. Her fat, dimpled arms braced her hands against her puffy face. Her voice sounded gruff and mean and her husband touched her arm as if to say, hey now.

I was so surprised, I nearly dropped my cup. Her rudeness brought my heart hammering against my ribs. And then I heard Chrissy's wheezing as she must have heard it. I'd become inured to the slight gurgling and since I knew it was a mainstay to CF, I didn't think about what others might think when they heard it.

The woman obviously thought Chrissy was very sick from the sounds coming from her. I remember that I turned to her slowly and forced a smile before saying very slowly, "My child has Cystic Fibrosis. She is not sick and I have no other choice if I want to put dry diapers on her." I nodded to the dryer. I gulped the rest of my coffee and turned away from them.

It happened often, the judgmental looks, the snide remarks about Chrissy because of her wheezing or coughing spasms. I had to grow tough skin during that time in our lives so I could focus only on her. And I tried to remember that everyone had a story that isn't written across their faces.

There was only one time when I wanted to punch somebody. We were in the grocery store. Chrissy was braced inside the cart and began coughing. I automatically held her close to wait it out like I usually did, giving her that warm touch that told her she wasn't alone. The coughing spasm was a hard one. She kept trying to smile at me between times and I must have smiled with the sad sweetness of it.

The woman beside me couldn't see Chrissy's face. When she heard her labored coughing and saw my smile, she slapped her hand against her cart handle. "What is the matter with you? Take that child home and give her some medicine. Or take her to the damned doctor. A loving mother wouldn't take her sick child into public places, especially a grocery store, to pass around germs. And why are you smiling, for God's sake? That child is sick!"

I was rattled and tried to count to ten before turning around to look at the woman. She had house slippers on and her coat hung crookedly over her heavy body. I saw no makeup, her hair was a rat's nest and her eyes glared at me. I'm not sure what got into me, but I stared her down and said, "Don't make assumptions. You don't know what you are talking about."

"Well, I know a sick child when I hear one." She stood up straight to get her point across.

This time I didn't bother counting to ten. "Mind your own business and I'll mind my own child." I gave her a look that said she should butt out. It should have turned her to stone since I thought that's what was inside her chest anyway.

"Well, I never…"

"Oh, I bet you did too…"

I left the woman sputtering behind us as I wheeled Chrissy away. I will never forget the look on her face or the way she gripped her pudgy hands around the coat, trying to pull it together. Her look of haughtiness followed me to the car. After I put the groceries inside with my daughter, I burst into tears.

CHAPTER FOURTEEN

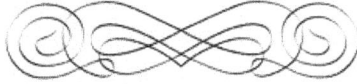

"I'll be right back, darlin'."

Christina grinned and slapped her hands on the high-chair tray. She was always in a good mood when she got up, for which I was continually thankful. I couldn't imagine what it would be like to have a cranky baby in the morning on top of her health issues. I dropped a kiss on the top of her head, put a couple of pieces of cut-up banana on the tray, which Christina eagerly snatched, and then I peeked out the window.

Dr. Grach had called earlier that morning. "Chrissy's lungs look very good. If I didn't know she had CF, I would say she looks like a normal child in every way."

I could hardly wait to tell Lance the good news. He was due home any minute. I was also excited because we were going to rent a real house instead of the duplex apartment next to the train tracks. Chrissy was trying to walk by then and it unnerved me to live near the creek behind us. Every time we went out the back door, she made a bee line for the water.

When I received the second phone call, I was over the moon with anxiety for him to get home. Linda had a new baby girl named Michele Lee. Everyone had been on pins and needles praying that she did not have Cystic Fibrosis. My stomach had been knotted with worry. And we were all blessed; Michele tested negative for CF. Chrissy had a new cousin and I hoped they could grow old together.

§

Chrissy decided she was tired of falling down, so by the first week of March she rounded the corner on her own two feet. We were both surprised, stared at each other and then she promptly fell on her butt. She scuttled across the floor toward me like a little crab. I picked her up, set her on her feet again and off she went...to her walker. She scooted it toward the door to the garage and stood there staring at me. Curious to see what she would do, I opened the door and she pushed it into the garage. I was stunned when she stretched to reach the knob and tried to close it again.

By the time her birthday arrived on March 15, she was walking like a little robot. She nearly ran into my mother's arms when they arrived and her birthday celebration began. A bunny cake, a pink coat and hat and a little black patent leather purse were memorable. And she ran her fingers over the dress I made for her, rubbed her face in the long-eared bunny from the Bergers and tried to open the locket from my Aunt Audrie who lived in Alaska. But her birthday cards were her favorites. She opened her gifts by tearing off the paper, looking at the contents and then she tossed them aside to finger the cards. Funny girl.

When the hullabaloo died down and everyone left, Chrissy was sick. Vomit and diarrhea, coughing and fevers. She wanted to be held continually as she pushed her warm face against my neck. Again my mind dove into overdrive. The flu or something else because of CF? As it turned out, the poor girl had the flu that lasted three days. As a young mother, I still had a lot to learn but I was getting the hang of it.

A month later, we'd fought away two more colds and Chrissy was now running everywhere. Walking wasn't good enough for her. She didn't realize that running caused more coughing. She'd stop and belly up to the couch, lay her head down and cough her little self to bits. Her face turned red and sweat drenched her golden hair to her head. When she finished, she'd heave a big sigh and take off again. It was the only life she knew, but it always broke my heart as I watched her struggling.

The astronauts were in trouble in space and everyone worried for their safety. We watched the television, hoping and praying. Chrissy could now reach the door knob to the back door easily. While we were watching the news about the astronauts, she was on her way outside. When the dog started barking, I jumped up and saw her headed toward the creek at a run.

Big sigh.

The astronauts were safe. Chrissy was safe. I was a mess. But I added one more event to my daily routine. Potty training. She looked at the potty and said *uh-oh*. She glared at the potty, sat down in the chair and I pulled the tray over her. Potty chairs in the early 70s consisted of a wooden chair with a removable potty beneath the seat. The tray fit over the child's head like an old wooden high chair. She promptly laid her head over her arms on the tray and fell asleep.

§

Chrissy wrapped her small arms around my neck and patted my back when I picked her up by then. Loving my child and remembering her little joys still brings tears to my eyes. She was loving from the time she felt the vibrations through her own heart.

Our lives were comparatively normal. We visited Mom and Dad in Portland some weekends and played pinochle late into the evening. My parents continued to overlook many of Lance's curious insecurities and I'm sure most of that was because they wanted to see Chrissy. I wasn't oblivious to the sometimes abrasiveness of the family situation, but so far, we were doing our best to compromise.

We went camping at Lost Lake near Hood River and when Mel Berger caught a fish and laid it on the table, Chrissy petted it like a kitten. Another time, we drove to the Astoria beach and she walked through the sand. I was adamant Chrissy live a normal life rather than raise her to die. The woman at the CF Foundation told me it was important that she live her life like other children. Chrissy enjoyed those days with loving people around her despite the constant coughing spasms before, during and after her postural drainage.

By the end of July 1970, I had to look for Lance in the late afternoon when I knew he'd rolled his truck into town a couple hours earlier. He was unhappy to leave his cronies or his beer, but I was determined to drag him home while he could still stand up. When he wanted to buy a new car, regardless of the sacrifices, I dug my feet into the sand. He was slipping back into his old ways and I was pedaling as fast as I could to hold on.

When CF Clinic day rolled around on July 28, I drove us toward Portland and the car broke down on the I-5 interstate. I was frantic. It was hot, I was alone and Chrissy was sick again. While I searched my brain for a solution, a semi-truck pulled up behind me. When the trucker walked up to my car window, my heart hammered and I made a quick decision.

Within some minutes, my daughter and I were in the passenger seat high above the road and a Good Samaritan was driving me to Portland. I left the car with a note on the windshield and held onto Chrissy tightly for safety. I trusted the man's sincere face and kind eyes, even though I know it could have been a catastrophe. He drove us to the Jubitz Truck Stop in Portland where he asked two of his friends to drive us to the CF Clinic on the hill. How could I trust all these strangers? I have no idea, but I was desperate and trusted my gut feelings. And I was right. They were mesmerized when Chrissy smiled at them despite her red-faced coughing.

We made it to the CF Clinic on time and Dr. Grach gave us antibiotics for Chrissy. Afterward, my Mom picked us up and we gave Chrissy a nap at her house, ate dinner and visited with my grandmother Terry who was visiting from Alaska.

Lance was livid when I told him I had left our car on the side of the freeway. "What were you thinking? Taking her with a truck driver. Now, how are you going to get home? That was a stupid thing to do." He ranted longer and grandma heard every word. My face turned hot. "What about my being on the side of the road with our baby alone in the heat?" When I saw grandma's eyes widen at his response, I hung up on him.

My Mom and Dad drove us home after dinner, but I wasn't looking forward to it and neither were they. Once we were in the house, they left again, obviously not wanting to talk with him any more than I did.

He was pacing back and forth as I put Chrissy to bed after the harrowing day; we were both exhausted. He followed me to her bedroom.

I glared at him and gave him the side eye.

"You should have stayed to wait for a cop. How could you get into that truck with a stranger? Someone could have vandalized my car."

"Really?! Someone could have vandalized the car."

He realized his mistake immediately and tried to back up. When his question slipped out, my eyes must have changed from tiredness to anger. I am shaking my head again as I write this story. Nobody could make this stuff up.

When the second shoe fell, I was almost prepared for it. I had seen the signs; I'd watched the beer cans pile up and Lance didn't come home during the day as often between his truck's bark chip loads. Again, naiveté blinded me. I'd seen him backsliding for about six weeks, but his drinking and many hangovers still didn't push me gone.

When Lance drove by in his truck, I waited two hours and he hadn't come home. We were expected at Linda and Stan's for dinner in Albany. I thought I would surprise him and push Chrissy in the stroller where he was going to pull his truck beneath the bark chip bins.

It was a beautiful day. As I walked, I inhaled the fresh air and hummed along the street. Chrissy was dressed like a princess. Tiny baby girls are such fun to dress. Unfortunately, it was me who got the surprise. As I rounded the corner, I saw his truck with its chrome wheels shining brightly in the lowering sun. I pushed the stroller towards the cab of the truck. It was empty. Shrugging, I turned to head toward the tavern, his favorite hangout.

That is when I saw Shelley's car parked beneath a shade tree a block away. My world collapsed again when I saw them together. They were in each other's arms and I thought I was going to vomit. I immediately turned Chrissy around and we walked swiftly home, around the truck, going the back way. My heart was pounding so hard that I could barely breathe. I hurried us inside the house and stood with my back braced against the front door, panting from the near-run.

I lifted Chrissy and looked into her unblinking gaze. Decision time.

Lance returned shortly after we did and he kept his eyes averted. I knew he had been drinking and I was disgusted. I knew how moody and sullen he could become when he drank. He knew there was an argument brewing, so he turned around and went back to the tavern before I could confront him. My stomach was in knots. I wanted to scream at him, beat my hands into his chest but it just wasn't the way I was built. I wanted softness, peace and calm.

What to do? Confront? Yell? Scream? I saw my neighbor outside and when she saw my face, she put her arms around me. Within minutes, my story spilled out and Helen found the nerve to tell me. Lance had been on the café's phone every day, which was a short walk from the bark chip filling station. She'd agonized over telling me, but she didn't want me to be blindsided. We'd become friends and she adored Christina.

Chrissy fell asleep. I had worked myself into a frenzy of anger. But when he came home again, I was afraid to confront him alone.

"We are supposed to be at your sister's for dinner."

He had forgotten "That's right. Let's go."

I was conflicted. Maybe having the last conversation at Linda and Stan's would be a better idea? "How about if I drive? Chrissy is asleep, but she'll fall asleep again when we start driving."

"I'm not drunk, babe…just happy," he grinned at me foolishly.

We didn't speak all the way to Albany. Chrissy did, indeed, sleep in my arms and my mind turned blank.

Linda gave me a quick hug and eyed me strangely, recognizing that something was terribly wrong. Dinner was strained as Lance boasted about his truck's fancy new wheels. My brother-in-law tried to slow down Lance's beer drinking. Stan rolled his eyes and Linda shook her head in confusion.

"Chrissy should be in bed. Let's go home." Suddenly, I did not want to involve them.

Lance wasn't happy, but once in the car, he seemed to quiet down and seemed curiously sober. But I was wrong.

Stupidly, I lashed out at him. "Lance, I saw you with Shelley."

He didn't respond except to white knuckle the steering wheel. He drove onto I-5 and stomped on the gas pedal so hard, we were nearly thrown into the door. I held Chrissy in my arms.

"You were spying on me. I didn't plan to see her. She was there and…It didn't mean anything. Honey, I'm still with you, aren't I?"

"What? It didn't *mean* anything?" I was wrong. He was drunk.

Sweet talking began in earnest as drunken words rolled into each other. He spouted more promises and told me Chrissy needed both parents. Really? Now he was thinking of her?

"Please don't throw us away." His blue eyes begged me to listen.

My brain slowly registered the speed of the car as we literally raced down the freeway. "Lance, slow down!" I was frightened. For myself, yes, but especially for Chrissy, who was being clutched so tightly in the shelter of my arms that she was crying loudly.

"Lance, you're crazy," I yelled at him.

He drove faster and turned up the volume of the country music that now blared into the car. I covered both of her ears with my hands. When I heard the police siren and saw the red and blue blinking lights behind us, I was so relieved I nearly cried. My hopes were dashed as suddenly as they were born when I saw that he meant to out-run the policeman. "Lance, slow down!" I screamed at him again.

"Hold on, babe. I can beat this cop. Watch me."

I crouched near the passenger door and clutched the armrest. I couldn't hold onto Chrissy, so I put her onto the floorboard wedged between my feet. Afterward, my feet and one hand held her while I struggled to hold onto the dashboard with the other. She was crying wildly and I scrubbed tears off my face.

Lance stomped down on the gas pedal harder and I saw the speedometer needle pass 100 mph as the police siren continued to wail behind us. "PLEASE LANCE, SLOW DOWN...SLOW DOWN...STOP THE CAR!" I screamed until my throat was raw. Chrissy was coughing by then and everything got blurry as the tears choked me.

The beer had dulled his brain and his mind snapped into a different place. Why did I confront him when I knew he was drunk? I asked myself then just as I ask myself now as I write about the event.

Lance looked over at me. "If you'd shut up, I know I can outrun this damn cop. You're the one who always says we can't afford things. Can you guess what a speeding ticket will cost?" He hauled the wheel around as he took the Turner exit on two wheels.

Fear swamped me. Chrissy cried louder. I couldn't catch my breath.

"Shut up!" He hit the brakes and we skidded half way across the graveled area. I was thrown into the car door. I whimpered and grabbed for Chrissy. The wild ride left me physically and mentally quaking inside even though I was relieved to stop.

The police car pulled alongside of us immediately. He was furious and after seeing me and Chrissy huddled in the corner of the car, I knew he wanted to grab Lance by the neck and choke him for his idiocy. He shook his head in amazement. The cop gave Lance a ticket and gave him a verbal lashing, using all the words that ran through my head.

Lance sounded sober when he answered him.

I closed my eyes and rested my head on the back of the seat, wondering if I should get out and walk the rest of the way home, clutching Chrissy to my breast. But of course, that was a stupid idea. It was late. It was dark. But I wanted out of that car.

The policeman made my decision for me when he said, "I am going to follow you the rest of the way home, buddy and you'd better not go a hair over 45 mph."

When we pulled away from the policeman, my relief was short-lived. Lance said through gritted teeth, "I could have lost that cop if you'd just kept your mouth shut."

I glared at him and lifted Chrissy in my arms. She was still whimpering when we parked and the policeman drove slowly away from us. Shaking and unsteady still, I knew I would leave in the morning. I was incensed and I screamed in my mind over and over again… I must get us away. I must.

Once inside, I didn't say one word. I clapped Chrissy, filled the mist tent and put her down to sleep. I slept on the couch.

"You'll get happy the same way you got mad," I heard him mutter the words and then the bed sagged beneath his weight. He started snoring immediately as if he hadn't a care in the world.

As I lay there, I made plans. We would leave before he returned from his last trip for bark chips. My spirit was finally broken.

Sometime during the night, he shook me awake.

"Come to bed."

I said, "Leave me alone."

He was still drunk. "No," he said angrily and became amorous. I slapped at him, tried to dodge him but he was stronger than I was. When he grabbed me and pulled me toward the bedroom, he pushed me down on the bed. I slapped at him again. He slobbered drunken kisses over me. I was repulsed. But, nothing I said could stop him.

Afterward, feeling completely numb, I did not say a word. I couldn't leave during the night, so I lay awake for hours packing everything in my mind as I waited for morning. Once he left for work I packed up the mist tent, all of Chrissy's CF paraphernalia, her baby food, her milk and two small suitcases. I wasn't fast enough though. He walked in during his morning break and surprised me. When he saw me pushing everything into my car, he was livid. When I didn't talk to him, but started to back the car out of the driveway, he yelled, "You won't be gone long! Oh, and you better take good care of my daughter."

I laughed at the irony of his words as I drove to Sally's house in Salem. I think, by then, I was almost relieved. My life had been a seesaw of emotions for months, even years. Being Chrissy's caregiver took all my stamina and most of my feelings. By this time, I could almost feel the burden of stress lift off and sail away out the car window. Maybe that was the day I became the woman I had yearned to be. Maybe I had stopped drinking the Lance Kool-Aid. Either way, I picked up that second shoe and tossed it away with both hands.

I was finally done and I allowed the shutters to drop on our marriage.

PART THREE

CHAPTER FIFTEEN

The chaos in our lives began to show in Chrissy's actions. Once we arrived at Mom's house the next day, she tried to claw her way out of her mist tent and pulled it down around her. Up until that day, she'd fallen asleep beneath the swirling mist without a hitch. The day we began our new life without Lance, changes began in the small things.

I headed back to the county offices and the woman gave me the third degree with all the questions. My record showed I had gone back and forth already and I feared that ADC might refuse my application this time.

As I sat there, my hand must have crept up to my neck, tapped my heart and the look of desperation on my face got through to them. I walked away with a check for $125. It doesn't sound like much, but in 1970, it helped me get started again.

Chrissy's anxiety showed up in whining, hiding from me and whimpering at nap time. At least she wasn't sick again, so I gave her space and when she saw I wasn't falling for her antics, she slowly began to smile after I gave her the pacifier again. She did not want to get into the car and I was sure she remembered the frightening night when she sat huddled on the floorboard.

The next day was a blur. I returned to Turner, packed up our things amidst Lance's wheedling for me to change my mind. After our last terrible encounter, I had trouble looking him in the eye. And I was furious that he pretended the rape hadn't happened at all. When he finally left, I could breathe again.

When his mother called me later that day as I scrambled to get our things into boxes, she told me Lance was drunk and raising hell. He was on his way back to Turner and she wanted to warn me to expect trouble. I thought I'd seen all the trouble he could give me, but I was wrong.

He arrived with tears in his eyes. He loved me and said he was a lost soul and why couldn't I see that? I did not bend in the wind.

Dad stayed in the background as he took boxes to his pickup and my car. When Dad was outside, Lance turned violent. He ripped the towel rod off the bathtub wall and pounded his fist into the wall for good measure. When he whirled around, I was shocked to see him grab Chrissy. He rushed out the door and jumped into his pickup truck and sped away before Dad could stop him.

I called the Turner Police and the Salem Police, frantic with worry. Lance was seen driving into his boss's driveway a couple miles down the road. Within minutes, he returned without Chrissy. He had a gun, but he couldn't find his bullets.

My heartbeat spiked. I couldn't think straight and Buzz, his boss, drove into the driveway with Chrissy in his arms. After a lot of tears and heart-stopping blips, I ran to open the door.

"Lance is violent. Please leave now." He gave Chrissy to me as if she were a cherished piece of china and hugged me goodbye. I saw pain and worry on his face. I held her and sobbed into her little chest.

Dad and I put Chrissy into the car and we left immediately.

The next few weeks passed us by as we cared for Chrissy as a team. It was wonderful to have my parents help. One nebulized, one clapped, one cooked, both of us cleaned and Chrissy enjoyed the peaceful change in the routine.

Lance called from time to time to ask how Chrissy was doing, careful not to blunder his way into our lives. For that, I was very relieved.

I did not ask him for child support because he was laid off once again. He seemed to accept the fact that I was never going to be part of his life again. Instead, he wanted to see Chrissy once in a while.

"You cannot take her anywhere in your car."

"I won't take her again. I promise."

"No you won't. Because you won't have her alone."

He didn't argue anymore.

Over the next months, I began selling Avon while Mom watched Chrissy in the afternoons after she got home from her own job. It was tedious, but at least I was earning some money. I knew I couldn't work at a secretarial job again with full-time hours because of Chrissy's needs, so Avon filled the spaces.

Chrissy liked the strolling walks when I made my deliveries and my customers looked forward to seeing my little assistant make her way up to their front door with their orders clutched in her hands. We made a game of it and Chrissy's vocabulary grew to include, "Avon Calling," in a little sing-song voice.

By the time Chrissy blew out her 2nd birthday candles, I was able to move us into an apartment a few miles south of Mom's house. She was delighted with the mailbox slot in our front door. When the mailman dropped our mail through the box, she clapped her hands and ran to retrieve the envelopes. Of course, I had to make sure they found their way into my own hands, so I wouldn't lose a bill or letter in one of her hiding places.

The day I hung curtains in her bedroom window, she sat on the bed to watch me. She was now sleeping in a twin bed and felt like a big girl. The side table was close to her bed, so I decided to step up on the bedrail and then stand on the lamp table to reach the curtain rod. When my foot slipped between the bed and the table, I was caught up by my kneecap and couldn't move. Pain shot up my leg and I yelped. Chrissy burst into laughter, sure I was entertaining her. Ugh. My knee was black and blue for a week and she kept touching it curiously with a confused look on her face.

During my life, I had attended several churches. Some I followed and some I did not. When I attended St. Mark's Episcopal Church in northwest Portland, I felt like I'd found my church home. Chrissy had not been baptized and neither had I, so I wanted to take care of that.

My biological father was Spanish and I was very close to my grandmother (abuelita). So, it was natural that in our family we often used some of the Spanish words I had grown up with. One of those words was "caca" which meant going potty. When the priest began to drop the holy water over her forehead as I held her in my arms, she kept trying to get down. When that didn't work, she said, "I have to go caca. I have to go caca." By this time, my brothers and family and I were trying our best not to laugh, but we just couldn't stop ourselves.

Afterward, the priest took me aside and asked me why we were laughing during such an important religious sacrament. When he heard my answer, his lips twitched and he patted Chrissy on the head.

My car was a 1962 Ford and barely functioning. My brothers had given me tires, but they were not new. The Bergers gave me two tires also to keep us safe. And then the battery kept dying. Mom and Dad had given me a AAA card, so if my car broke down, all I needed to do was call the number on the back of the card and help would come.

It began to be a joke. When the car wouldn't start, Chrissy would say, "Call Triple A, Momma."

I'd call and a man would come over with jumping cables. The car would start, Chrissy would clap her hands and we would drive away. It was nearly a ritual and her sense of humor amazed me. She was about two and a half years old by then. One day we were going to the CF Clinic and my car wouldn't start. She told me to call Triple A; the man arrived with cables in hand. While we sat in the car, he pulled up the hood. When he looked around the hood at us with a chuckle, I didn't know what was wrong.

"Oh, miss. I can't charge your battery this time."

"Why not?"

"Because someone stole your battery."

"What?"

We laughed; the thief wouldn't get far with it. Chrissy couldn't understand what was going on. She put both hands on her hips when we got out of the car. She looked at the man and said, "Our car won't go."

He burst out laughing and drove away. Mom and Dad came to the rescue again. I had a new battery that afternoon and we made it to the CF Clinic just a little late. When we arrived, Chrissy told Dr. Grach we lost our battery and needed a new one.

Most of my furniture was stored in my brother's garage nearby. When I needed something, I dug through boxes. One day, a man from a finance company called to say he had a repossession order and would arrive in two days. He listed my car, the couch, chair, sewing machine, and Chrissy's crib. What? I had no idea who he was or what finance company he was calling from. After some discussion, I learned that Lance had forged my signature when he bought his fancy yellow pickup truck and listed our furniture as collateral. How in the world this could happen, I have no idea. I argued, but nothing worked.

My couch was in good shape. My brother Rick's was old and battered. We exchanged couches and I gave the financier his address. When he arrived at Mom's house with the old couch to pick up everything else, Mom and I were sitting on the front porch waiting for him.

"There is my car. You have my couch, chair and tables. You will not take away my child's bed or my sewing machine."

The man studied us and decided not to argue. His assistant took my keys and they both drove away. Now I didn't have a car. Although we were proud of ourselves, I wanted to punch out Lance's lights once again.

§

Several days later, Lance was inducted into the U.S. Army again.

Time was running out and I wanted a divorce before he left for Vietnam. The divorce lawyer was downtown and he prepared the papers to serve Lance before he left. Too much time had elapsed since I started the order and I wasn't sure I could divorce him when he was out of the country, but I did. I went to court and sighed happily when he didn't show up.

By the end of 1971, I had a part-time receptionist job downtown. Selling and delivering my Avon products was exhausting and sporadic. With a regular paycheck, I was able to hold my head up high again. From there, I changed to another part time job earning more money. Chrissy had a day care woman who watched her. We managed to clap her before, after and nighttime with the hours I worked. Life was better for both of us. It had just taken me nearly three years to make it happen.

Chrissy enjoyed the snow at Christmas and we'd passed the year without any major health issues. My brothers learned how to clap her in an emergency. She swallowed the foul-smelling pancreatic granules in tubs of apple sauce and still smiled through it all.

During those many months between leaving Lance and Turner behind, I told myself that I didn't need a man in my life. I didn't need a man to complete me. I was whole. Chrissy was my life now, just as I'd dreamed she would be during the nine months I carried her. Now it was our turn. I had to regain my confidence and concentrate on Chrissy.

Six months later, that vow turned to mush when I met Frank Zaccone on a blind date/birthday party. My friend's cousin was home on leave from Vietnam. When I walked into that party, I saw him across the room and thought, "Wow, I hope that's him." It was and my life was turned upside down.

CHAPTER SIXTEEN

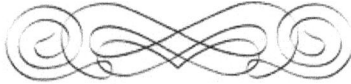

It was a whirlwind romance that took place in two weeks. Frank returned to Vietnam and we wrote letters back and forth like teenagers for six months. I think he fell in love with Chrissy first.

I continued to work and keep my daughter healthy as we counted the days before Frank returned in the spring. By then, it was decided that we would marry and move to Youngstown, Ohio. Mom and Dad were sad as they were extremely close to Chrissy, but I made the choice to change our lives and hoped for a brighter future. Chrissy would have a step-father.

Dr. Thomas Boat at the Cystic Fibrosis Clinic in Cleveland, Ohio received all of Chrissy's medical records and we made plans to visit the clinic once we arrived in Ohio in June of 1972.

Frank married both of us, as Chrissy would tell everyone. We enjoyed the feeling of family. She had a wedding dress just like Momma, so she got married too, right? Frank was called Daddy. She barely remembered Lance. He was an amazing father to her and I knew I had made the right decision to move away from my family and create one of my own.

The Zaccone clan accepted Chrissy into their fold and his huge Italian family became ours. She had a cousin her age named Dawn and they were soon inseparable playmates. Frank's Aunt Violet taught me to cook Italian, his friend made Italian red wine that was stronger than anything I'd ever drank. Oh, I learned to drink only one glass after the first imbibing. When I got into the car after two glasses, I couldn't hold the car still as it twirled around and around. Yep, one glass was enough for the entire evening from then on.

Chrissy flourished.

Until she didn't.

Dr. Boat suggested a week in the University Hospital adjacent to the Cystic Fibrosis Clinic. The heat and humidity was hard on her as she fought for breath in the muggy atmosphere. Although we had a window air conditioner, the air was sticky and unbearable. Sleeping inside her mist tent added another layer of discomfort and within a few months, her coughing was worse.

"A week?" I was stunned with the thought.

Dr. Boat looked apologetic. "Yes, with CF children, it is often necessary to do a cleaning-out procedure because their lungs are so clogged up that they need a bit of help with their daily lives." He was gentle with Chrissy and she understood a little of what he was telling us.

"I don't want to." Her voice shook. She was nearly four years old and she'd already undergone a hospitalization a few months earlier to correct a lazy eye. She'd worn small blue-framed glasses from the time she was two, and the surgical procedure had pulled the eye muscle taut and she was thrilled to see without glasses. But she hadn't liked being in the hospital in Youngstown. She knew the drive between our home and Cleveland was a long way. I felt her shudder at the thought.

When we had to leave her in the hospital, it broke my heart because she was so stressed. Chrissy handled stress differently than I did; she ignored those around her and refused to be pulled into conversations. Her eyes were accusing when I hugged her goodbye and she just watched us leave without a word.

That week was hard on all of us.

She started peeing the bed and the doctor said, "Do not reprimand her. It is the only way she can fight back. I've seen this happen many times. We will keep her clean, therapists work on her with postural drainage five or six times a day. Coughing up that phlegm will clean her out. She is doing well, even though she doesn't think so. She doesn't talk much and keeps to herself, but now she is coloring pictures and has made friends with her bedmate. Max also has CF, so she realizes she is not alone."

I remember the day she introduced us to Max, a boy two years older than her who was in the bed beside her. She grinned at me for the first time in nearly a week that day. When Max had the packing removed from his sinus area the day before, Chrissy had cried with him. She seemed to take on everyone else's pain and make it her own. For a child so young, I was constantly amazed with the way she handled life.

When Frank first came into her young life, Chrissy was fearful of loud noises and very shy of strangers. Within two years, she yelled outside with the other children, she talked to everyone and showed a distinct independent streak. Basically, she felt secure and he made it so.

When she was four years old, we lived in an apartment house across the hall from another little girl about her age. They played daily, but when I listened to them, Chrissy seemed to want control of the playtime and the conversation. One day, she sounded disgruntled and I heard her say, "Jenny, I hear your mother calling you."

When Jenny ran across the hall, Chrissy closed the front door and locked it. I was perplexed.

"I didn't hear Rose call Jenny."

She looked at me impishly and grinned. "I wanted her to go home."

"What? You stinker." It was hard to keep a straight face when I saw Chrissy's hands covering her mouth, trying to hold in giggles.

Frank taught Chrissy to face her fears with his patience and understanding. He adored her and she returned that love fervently. She didn't know Lance. He rarely wrote or called; he had disappeared like a phantom but agreed for Frank to adopt Chrissy.   She told total strangers her name was now Chrissy Zaccone.

She didn't think me, me, and me. She was always in the middle of things and her sensitivity to others surprised me because she was so very young. She was a conversationalist and often talked non-stop.

By that fall, when my sister-in-law had a baby girl, she was happy to have a new cousin. After Chrissy held Angelina, she said, "I think I need a baby brother, Momma."

Frank and I laughed at her. But she was very serious. "I want Santa to bring me a baby brother," she repeated.

"Well, babies need more than three months to grow," I told her as I smiled at her intensity.

"Oh. Well, when can we start to make one grow?"

"Chrissy. You are a funny little girl."

"I know, Momma. That's why you love me, right?"

When she raised her eyebrows at her statement, I couldn't help but laugh and we were soon giggling like children. "I guess so," I murmured.

By the time Christmas time arrived, I knew I was pregnant. I am unsure if I was more anxious to tell my husband or my daughter she would have a baby brother or sister in eight months.

She was delighted and immediately began moving her toys around in her bedroom. When I asked her what she was doing, she said, "Well, where is my baby brother going to sleep and play? I have too much stuff." Although I tried to tell her she had a long time before it would matter, she pushed boxes of toys under her bed and in the closet. She also told everyone we met in the grocery store and at family gatherings that she was going to be a big sister. When I told her she could tell grandma and grandpa our news on the telephone, one would have thought I had given her the moon.

We moved into a house which was larger than the apartment and there was a back yard. Girard was a smaller town near Youngstown and

Chrissy was delirious with joy because there were playmates on both sides of us. No more apartment living. She, again, scooped her things to make room for a baby brother that was "growing in Momma's tummy."

The local mall advertised that Santa Claus would be in a trailer in the parking lot that year. I was sure Chrissy would like visiting Santa. She kept up a running conversation trying to imagine herself with the big man. She would ask questions and then answer herself. When I started laughing at her self-conversations, she pulled her eyebrows tight and pursed her lips.

"Will he give me a present?"

"No, probably not."

"Why?"

"He will probably give you a candy cane if you're good."

She thought about it before responding, "Well, if he doesn't have presents, he'll be sorry…"

"No," I said. "YOU'LL be sorry."

And of course, with a candy cane in her hand later that day, she was still smiling all the way home. She'd forgotten all about our conversation.

I was a seamstress. Mom had taught me from an early age and sewing for Chrissy was always a treat. When I learned how to knit, I created a yellow skirt and vest for her. It was just one of many outfits I would make for September when she would begin kindergarten. Since we now lived 2,500 miles from Mom and Dad, we wrote letters and sent photos. During that year while I was pregnant, I sewed school clothes because I knew once my baby was born, I wouldn't have as much time. And it also kept my mind away from the worries of a possible CF child. Although I knew both parents had to be carriers, there was no test at that time to know if Frank carried the recessive CF gene. So, I sewed, cooked and played with her to keep my mind occupied.

By the end of June, we were kept inside the house because of the intense heat and humidity. There was a tiny store at the end of our block with a soft ice-cream machine. We walked up to get an ice cream cone nearly every day (that probably led to my weighing 165 by the time my baby was born). She started preparing for her cone about ten o'clock daily.

She loved to sing along with me when songs we knew came on the radio. Since Elvis was my favorite, she learned the songs and kept up with me. Often, we'd pretend to be in a singing contest to see who made a slip first. Invariably Chrissy won and we'd end up in laughter.

The song on the radio that caught her fancy was "Tie a Yellow Ribbon Round the Ole Oak Tree." She knew all the words and we sang along with the radio, each of us trying to sing above the other. To this day, when I hear Tony Orlando and Dawn sing that song, I get choked up and when I sing along like I did in the old days, my eyes leak.

My parents flew to Ohio for a visit in July and Chrissy nearly fainted with glee when Dad and Frank set up the swing set in our back yard. We knew she needed something out there because the weeks before they arrived, I was sewing down in the basement while she played with Robbie next door. What I didn't know was that day Robbie had returned home and she stayed outside playing. Chrissy had climbed the tree in our back yard and was stuck there and couldn't get down again.

I heard her yelling, "Momma, Momma…" And then she'd laugh. When I finished the seam, I ambled my pregnant body upstairs and outside. When I saw her dangling from the tree limb with one leg and one arm wrapped around the tree, I started laughing. When she saw me laughing, she started laughing again and I barely caught her before she hit the ground.

One day my neighbor Maggie called and asked to speak with Chrissy. A little perplexed, I handed her the phone.

"Yes." Chrissy whispered. "No. I'll ask Momma."

She handed me the phone to hang up and bit her lip.

"What's going on?"

"I need to go over to Chris's house to clean up something."

"...Oooo-kay. Do you want to tell me about it?"

She thought a minute before saying, "No."

I walked her next door and Maggie met us at the door. Her son Chris had a bucket and two sponges. He solemnly handed one to Chrissy and they walked upstairs into their attic. When the children were out of earshot, Maggie pulled me into the living room and started laughing.

"Those kids were coloring upstairs. When I went up there later, I saw that they hadn't colored on paper. They colored on the walls. Chrissy drew giant Zs and Chris drew giant Ps for their last names, Zaccone and Peduzzi. The funny part of that is Chris's P was above the Z because he was just that much taller. They colored their letters as far as they could reach. All the way around the room on four walls."

I rolled my eyes. "Let's have some coffee. They'll be up there a while." I took a big breath and then we were both laughing again.

Chrissy started kindergarten on September 4, 1974. We'd taken a photo op of her in each of her new outfits to send to grandma and grandpa in Oregon. She was poised to begin school, with a book bag, pencils, crayons and a delirious excitement that mounted each day.

When I went into labor the next day to make her a big sister to her little brother, Frankie, her priorities wavered. When we brought him home from the hospital a week later, she wanted to quit school to take care of him.

Her little girlfriend came over to play and see the new baby brother. We had the same bassinet Chrissy used as a baby and she would not allow her friend to bend over the crib unless she stood close by. Frank and I were amused by her proprietary actions, but it wasn't until our sister-in-law Debi came to visit that we realized how far she'd go to retain ownership of him.

Debi held Frankie while Chrissy sat next to her on the couch. When Debi pulled the blanket away from his face, Chrissy promptly pushed it back. When Frankie whimpered, Chrissy told Aunt Debi to put him on her shoulder and pat his back like I did.

A few minutess later, Chrissy said, "I think Momma needs to change Frankie. I smell peepee."

Debi laughed. "I can change him."

"No, I think Momma needs to do that."

"Really? You don't think I can do it?"

"Well, you don't have a baby, so..." Debi laughed again.

"Can I hold him now?" Her arms reached outward.

"Chrissy, you can hold your brother any time and Aunt Debi is just visiting us today. You can hold him again when Aunt Debi goes home."

She sighed loudly and looked up into Debi's face. "Aunt Debi, when are you going home?"

That little imp did not want to share her baby brother with anyone. And she didn't want to go back to school. She became his protector and ran for diapers, powder, or up and down the stairs to the basement if I hadn't brought up his clothing when we needed them.

She was mesmerized when I nursed him and placed her elbows on the side of my chair staring and listening to him guzzle down his milk. One time her nose got so close that Frankie's arms raised up to grab her nose. When she giggled, Frankie let go of my nipple with a popping sound. At that point, Chrissy curled up on the floor laughing so hard that the ever-present coughing started. I was sitting there with my boob hanging out, one child on my lap and trying to reach down to sooth the other at the same time. At this point, I laid the baby on the floor, Chrissy abruptly stopped coughing and decided it was play time.

One day when Frankie was about a month old, I could see something was on her mind. She followed me into the bedroom after I nursed him, tailed me to the cupboard to pull out diapers and then his clothes. As I prepared him for a nap, I studied her and after placing him into the crib, I saw her face. She shook her head and stared at Frankie through the crib railing.

"Momma, where is Frankie's mist tent?"

I froze, unsure how to answer her. And then I turned to her and said, "Frankie doesn't have a mist tent. You have one because you have CF." And then I caught my breath, afraid of her response.

Her forehead creased in thought. She stared at him again through the railings and then back at me. "And Frankie doesn't have CF like me?"

I tried not to cry while I nodded my head no. I had no idea what she would say or do next and hoped I had the strength to answer her.

She threw her small arms around my legs and hugged my knees. She was crying. Before I could say anything further, she said, "I'm so happy that Frankie doesn't have CF too! And no mist tent and no coughing and no pills and…" She began to blubber into my legs and I just sat on the floor and pulled her into my arms to let her cry it out. There are no words to describe that day when her little body shuddered in my arms.

CHAPTER SEVENTEEN

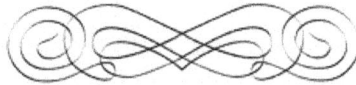

As it turned out, Chrissy loved every minute of school time. She loved to write her name. She could count to one hundred and say her ABCs. Whenever I tried to help her with school work, she'd say, "I can do it myself, Momma." She was thoroughly ready for class and the stories she shared with us when she came home always gave us a laugh.

We were happy the hot, humid weather started to cool off and she could play outside again. Her spurts of coughing was mostly when she had a cold, so it was a normal little girl who flit next door to play with either Chris or Robbie on the other side. She and both boys played well together and our lives were good.

I had a seamstress business from home and always had too much work. My cash box was always full and I began to save that money for some day. I loved sewing and it seemed like the perfect job. I could stay home and customers came to me.

It was about that time when Chrissy was nearly six and Frankie was six months old that Frank was becoming very unhappy with his job at the Erie Lackawanna Railroad. He'd worked there for some time, so when he returned from Vietnam, we married and he returned to his job. He felt it was a dead-end job and wanted a change.

His parents lived in Idaho and mine lived in Oregon, so it seemed like an easy decision to move west. We had many friends in Ohio, especially Chuck and Gloria, who we would miss terribly. But, the die was cast. Dad told Frank he could probably get a job at the welding shop where he worked. So, we made plans, packed up, hired a moving van and sent it ahead of us.

Mom and Dad had bought a house next door, so their house was now a rental and it was available. Life seemed to be moving in the right direction. We would both be near our parents. Chrissy could be back with Dr. Grach at the CF Clinic again and begin first grade in Portland.

I had saved up my sewing money and it paid for our trip to Portland. During that long road trip, I came down with the flu. Of all times to get sick, I couldn't believe our luck. Instead of sharing the driving west, Frank did most of it because every time I got behind the wheel, I got sleepy and nauseous.

Frankie was ten months old by the time we arrived in Portland. Chrissy was happy to see her grandparents again. I was glad to see my parents again and moving next door was a bonus.

As I introduced my son to his grandparents for the first time, Chrissy had been coaxing him to walk for several days. When I turned around to get Frankie, Chrissy was again trying to get him to walk toward her. And he did. We were all stunned to see that little guy head toward his big sister with a grin on his face, step, step, step.

Welcome to Portland. I thought that was my only surprise.

But I was wrong.

Frank went to work where my Dad was employed, but he had been laid off his job within the first two weeks. We were upended. He began looking for a new job.

In the meantime, my flu turned out to be something entirely different. Back in Ohio when I missed my period, the doctor said it was normal for it to be sporadic after birthing a child. He also said I could not get pregnant when I was nursing. Then, he said I had a small cyst on my ovary and to see a gynecologist when I arrived in Portland.

I made the appointment. When I explained what my Ohio GYN had told me, my new doctor raised his eyebrows and had me pee in a cup.

When he told me I was pregnant, I went into shock mode. Pregnant again??

Mom and I got into the elevator, both shell shocked. When the doors opened, we realized we'd forgotten to punch in the button for the first floor. When I got home, Frank was ecstatic. I was still in shock. I'd just lost all my baby weight and imagined going to work to get us on our feet. The idea of being pregnant again so soon had not been on my agenda at all.

But my disappointment at being pregnant changed when I started bleeding and I feared a miscarriage. I wanted this baby and after all the drama in my previous life, I was going to save it. I went to bed for three days and took care of Frankie as well as I could with my Mom's help.

My little girl, Audrie, was born seven months later. The night before she was born, Dad had taken me to the Elks Father/Daughter Banquet. He'd teased me about having the baby on his watch and I knew I still had about ten days to go. I was wrong. My water broke during that night and my girl was born the next morning. My children were seventeen months apart.

Chrissy was dancing a jig. A baby brother and baby sister. How could life get any better? She was following me like a shadow trying to help me be a Momma. She kept Frankie busy while I nursed Audrie and played with him when I needed a break. She carried Audrie around like a doll until I explained that she might drop her. What? She said, "I would never drop my baby sister." She looked shocked that I would think such a thing could happen.

The day she asked me if Audrie had CF, I was more prepared for it than I was when she asked me about Frankie.

She looked at me sideways while I was changing Audrie. "Momma, she's like Frankie, isn't she?"

At first, I was confused by her question. But when I saw the serious look on her face, I knew what she was asking me. "CF?"

"Uh-huh. She won't need a mist tent either, will she?"

I could see tears brewing in her eyes. I pulled her close to me. "Audrie had a test at the hospital. Remember when I told you that CF babies taste like salt when you kiss their foreheads?"

She nodded solemnly.

"Do you want to give her the test, sweetheart?"

Chrissy's eyebrows rose and she looked between me and her baby sister. Without a word, she leaned over and kissed Audrie's forehead and I saw her tongue dart out quickly to taste the baby's brow.

The smile on her face when she turned to me brought tears. It glowed with love and excitement and joy. I'd never seen the look on her face before. Then, she leaned down, hugged Audrie and nuzzled her baby cheek with her own.

"Oh, good." She whispered.

I swallowed the lump in my throat and thanked God that my two babies would never have to go through the clogged lungs, forced coughing, stinky granules or the various calamities that their big sister had lived through and accepted as a given.

Her greatest delight was making Audrie and Frankie laugh, helping me cook in the kitchen, helping fold clothes from the dryer, writing letters and eating.

CHAPTER EIGHTEEN

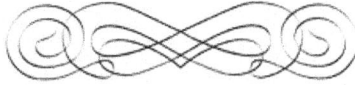

Chrissy grew and blossomed as each season blended into the next. With CF, she became used to pills, mist tents, respiratory therapy and other children teasing her. But through it all, she was a child that couldn't seem to be spoiled.

Chrissy's school days were at Laurelhurst School in northeast Portland. She had a lot of friends in school, some closer than others. When she had a coughing spasm at school, her friends came to her rescue to fend off those others who mimicked her coughing as if it was a joke. The teachers tried to keep the children civil, but we all know that children can be cruel.

One day when she was in the second grade she had her first real face off. That was the day she felt different. She began to hold back her coughs because the children teased her sometimes. Instead of coughing, she held her breath and tried to clear her throat to avoid humiliation. She didn't want to be embarrassed in front of her peers and friends. It was about that time that she started asking me why she had to cough at all.

The day when she came home, quiet and withdrawn, brought up my antennae. It was like pulling teeth to get the story from her compressed lips. The words tumbled out as she swayed toward me. I held her and squeezed her close as I listened to the story. A boy at school pretended to cough every time she was forced to do so. After lunch, her friends rallied around her and proceeded to knock the boy to the ground. Chrissy couldn't cope with the angst. I also found out she'd been skipping her pancreatic enzymes at lunch time because they teased her about that too.

"The teacher was talking to him when I left class." She started sobbing with the unfairness of it all and I couldn't let go of her.

The boy sought her out the next day and apologized. As it turned out, from that day forward, that boy became her loyal knight. Anyone who was even suspected of teasing her about anything had him to reckon with. We wondered what on earth the teacher told the boy to make him so thoughtful. But we didn't care. Her life eased up a bit afterward.

When she took the Iowa test, her teachers were stunned when she passed with nearly straight As. She carefully wrote her letters, studied hard and listened to her teacher like a lifeline to the future. She also was sometimes reprimanded for telling her fellow students how to work out their problems. The teachers reminded her that was why they were in the room.

One of her habits was to touch everything and to use her finger to taste everything. She was stubborn, but assumed her sense of humor would keep her out of mischief. Sometimes it worked, sometimes it didn't. If there was chip dip, she'd dip in the finger. If there was spaghetti sauce, she'd dip in the finger. When her grandma or I made chocolate chip cookies, yes, she'd dip in the finger.

One day, she tried it and I snapped the wooden spoon toward her finger. She jumped and then quickly jabbed it in again. This time, I had the laugh because she'd stuck her finger into the wet yolk of an egg. It slowed her down but didn't stop her.

When she was in the third grade, she found an old photo album that showed her in a little pink dress on her first birthday in Turner, Oregon. Suddenly, she burst into tears and slammed the photo album shut.

When I came to find out what happened, she turned to me and said through tears, "Why didn't my Daddy love me?"

She'd seen photos of Lance. She knew he was her biological father and she'd heard he had remarried and had another child. She felt strange and sad because nobody had answers for her.

When the Bionic Woman series was on the television, she loved the program. She'd often copy her by gently pushing some of her golden hair behind one ear and pretending her bionic ears could "hear" far away. She was such a funny girl. Sometimes she'd stop us when we were doing something and say, "Oh, wait." And she'd push that hair and raise an eyebrow as if hearing a secret nobody else could hear.

When Charlie's Angels was on the television, she transferred her allegiance to Farrah Fawcett. And she wanted her hair style. She wanted to look just like her. So, we got out my scissors and I cut and shaped it into a Farrah look. And then we went next door to grandma's house, who got out the camera.

She was very close to Mom and Dad. Since we lived next door, she was often on their doorstep. It was a running joke when she'd show up and Dad would say, "Hey, don't you have a home?" His eyes would twinkle and she'd get a big hug.

She left her mark on her drawings and I would often find her sitting at the dining room table with her pencils and crayons drawing pictures for either Frankie or Audrie. And then she put them into books.

When Audrie was old enough to sit in the infamous walker that Chrissy used to nearly cripple me, she would lie on the floor beneath her baby sister and talk to her. Audrie would lean over the walker and grin at her, often drooling and slobbering all over her. Chrissy would wipe off her face with a sleeve and continue her giggling conversation. It was as if her sister and brother were put on earth just for her entertainment.

Pneumonia and maintenance work took her to the hospital off and on during those days. Sometimes she would stay a week, sometimes more or less days. She loved the nurses because they loved her and soon had them doing her bidding. She helped them with art work when they decorated the glass enclosures at Doernbecker Hospital, pushed smaller children up and down the halls, had them read stories to her and generally had a party time during each sojourn.

But she still hated hospitals. She hated white. She hated shots. She hated medicine. She liked the nurses and most of the doctors. She liked the food in the hospital because she didn't have to finish everything on her plate. She disliked the postural drainage because it made her cough. And of course, she hated coughing. She didn't use the word hate because it was one of the taboo words in our household, but I knew her feelings just the same. She hated CF and everything related to it.

Instead, she liked to concentrate on reading books, writing stories, playing at the park a block from our house and harvesting grandma's strawberries next door. She also spent time with Frank, especially when he had a dish of popcorn, ice cream or any other snack; she would sidle up to him and dip in a finger.

When she needed discipline, we would only have to talk to her and her lips would quiver and she'd fight back tears. Those big blue eyes would fill up and glaze over. It worked every time. No spankings needed for our girl. One or two words and she was mush. And so were we.

She had several girlfriends when she was in the third grade, especially Patty and Jody. I was the Brownie Scout Leader and my sister-in-law Sheryl was my aid. She played the guitar and sang songs. The girls were enamored with her.

I remember one of their special songs was Puff the Magic Dragon. It's hard to type the name of the song because the lyrics run through my head as I hear Sheryl's voice and then Chrissy's voice joins her. One day about two years ago, the song came on my radio as I was driving through Phoenix. All of a sudden, I started crying and had to pull off the road to sob my tears out. It is hard to believe how the sounds of a song can put you right back to that moment in time, but it surely can do that. I wanted to nestle down into sweet oblivion where pain didn't live.

By this time in Chrissy's life, her stomach was slightly distended because her food was not digested easily like normal children's. The pancreatic pills she swallowed with each meal helped, but nothing could alleviate the tummy distension. She was a small girl with thin arms and legs, but overall by the fall of 1977 she looked as normal as a girl her age could appear, albeit small.

I saw her face wreathed in smiles most days and I often wondered what she had to smile about when CF loomed daily in her life in a never ending cycle of regimen. I was angry that she had to live through the stress of it all, but mostly she seemed to take it in her stride even though at times I could see the distress on her face.

She hid her negative feelings from her Dad and grandpa. She could share it with me and grandma, but otherwise she put on a good face. To see a child try to shield an adult seemed backwards to me. Usually, it was the other way around.

When she walked, she had a lilt in her stride except those times after a severe coughing spasm. It was then that she coughed and twisted her arms around her belly, bend over and cough until her face was pink with sweat. Her hair was wet beneath her bangs and often clung to the back of her neck during these bouts. She didn't smile then.

On her good days which were most days, she liked her clothing to match. She was a clothes diva at eight years old. Her socks had to match her blouse or her pants had to match her blouse or sweater. She was a walking fashion show. I think she took after my grandmother Myrtle Terry, who never wore a short-sleeved sweater with her slacks unless her socks matched her top.

Since I had spent so much time with Chrissy before Frankie and Audrie were born and then later, she spent so much time with my Mom, her vocabulary was immense. It was strange to hear an eight year old use words such as absolutely, especially, completely, misunderstand, to note a few.

She often used her hands to make a point and we teased her unmercifully. Now that I think about this, I realize she was mimicking me. When she saw me talk to others, I did the same thing. Funny about the mannerisms our children have and we don't see the forest for the trees. So, I knew where she picked that up.

Many in our family used to say she was a little old woman in a child's body. She did not always like being teased because she wanted others to take her seriously. However, when some of her conversations became too deep and she knew she had an audience, her chatter box gene took over. And then her hands would fly around her head, across in front of her and people soon lost track of the conversation altogether.

I remember how she'd bubble with laughter when anyone held down her hands to see if she could still talk without them.

CHAPTER NINETEEN

Chrissy felt defeated at times because she couldn't run fast with her friends or take ballet lessons. She shrugged her shoulders though, because she avoided the coughing that always followed her. She played hopscotch instead. She wanted to play tether ball and tried it once. The over exertion made her chest hurt and produced a coughing spasm.

Then there was the spelling bee. She won a place in her class to be on the KPBS Radio Spelldown with other students across the city of Portland. It was a small radio station and parents were asked to allow the children to ride on the school bus. We essentially were not invited to be part of the audience. We turned on the radio to listen and we waited expectantly. When Chrissy's turn came, she and another boy were the only students left standing at the end. We knew she would win. She was a wordsmith and knew her stuff. All of a sudden, I heard Chrissy's voice become raspy and I knew she was trying to suppress a cough. It sounded like she had a "frog" in her throat and I ached for her. She concentrated so hard on not coughing that she missed a word that was very easy for her. She lost, of course. I heard her coughing as the winner's name was called over the air. Later she told me she felt stupid.

Summer camp? Absolutely not.

I was conflicted when Dr. Grach suggested Cystic Fibrosis Summer Camp for a week. It was about an hour from home eastward and my first thoughts were, no. I did not want her traipsing off into the forested areas with a group of children. What if someone was sick and she came home with an infection? What if she was afraid to go so far from home without me? What if…what if….?

"How can you worry about Chrissy when she will be in a camp filled with people who are trained to care for CF children?"

I did not have a good answer.

"And she will have postural drainage during the day."

"Uh-huh…"

Dr. Grach could see I was weakening, so she came in for the kill. "And don't you think it would be wonderful if she was around a group of children who all had CF instead of being the only one in the crowd like she is at school? Everyone coughs. Everyone gets clapped. Everyone swallows enzyme pills with their food…and…"

I laughed and put a hand on the woman's arm. "Okay…okay."

When Frank and I dropped her off at camp on the Monday morning and the children scampered around her, Chrissy was hesitant and did not want to let go of my hand.

We knew we would return on Wednesday afternoon for a parent visit, so we reluctantly left her in the appointed cabin as she fought tears to see us go. Two days later, we arrived --- fully expecting to hear that she wanted to return home with us early. We had, of course, missed her.

When the counselor pointed toward her cabin where she shared the room with five other children, we walked inside to find her sitting in a circle with her cabin mates.

We called her name. She looked up, waved a dismissive hand and said, "Oh, hi Mom and Dad." And then she resumed the game. We were stupefied and delighted…and maybe just a little bit disappointed? Probably. When she got home that week from camp, she chattered endlessly about the fun, the friends, the food and being in the wilderness.

When another one of Chrissy's colds put her into the hospital at Doernbecker when she was seven years old, she didn't want to stay. The doctor promised her she would only be there a few days, she still wasn't happy. One day, an artist arrived on the children's floor to draw a picture of the patients because it cheered most of them up. Since Chrissy was not happy to be there and her way of fighting back was to ignore everyone, she told him to draw other kids, just not her. He was amused, but sat in the doorway to draw her anyway. Frank and I had a good laugh when we saw the picture on the wall afterward; she wore her Raggedy Ann pajamas and her face was studiously ignoring the man. When I asked her about it, she said, "I told him not to draw a picture of me, so I watched cartoons until he went away." It was one of the most beautiful drawings of Chrissy that I had ever seen. I never met the artist to thank him, but the nurses told me he was very amused at her response to him. She kept giving him the side eye to see if he was still there. Neither said a word. When he was finished, he quietly went into her hospital room, taped it to the wall and saluted her as he left. She still ignored him.

Our vacations usually took us from Portland, Oregon to Hagerman, Idaho where Frank's parents Joe and Josephine Zaccone lived. It was a very small town and every summer, the big family reunion was usually held around Frank's Dad's birthday the end of June. The children always had a good time because they lived across from the school yard and on the other side there was a large park. And swimming.

When the Zaccone and Arterburn families gathered together, there were too many children to count. And Chrissy tried to keep up with all of them. At night, grandpa Zaccone pulled out his large telescope to point out the stars to children and adults alike. Chrissy adored him and stuck to him like glue most of the time. He treated her like she was his own grandchild and it endeared me to him and Mom to see them love my child that much.

This photo was taken June 1977 and the sprinkler had drenched the kids as they ran through it all afternoon. Chrissy's bout of coughing kept her sitting and Frankie and Audrie seemed to gravitate to her and wanted to sit with her even while they watched their cousins and friends slip and slide through the water. It always amazed me to see their camaraderie with each other and when she wasn't hovering over them, they were following her like a shadow.

By the fall of 1977, pneumonia put her in the hospital again. It was just before Audrie's second birthday. She wanted to be part of the birthday party, so we took the party to the Good Samaritan Hospital. There we went with cake, candles, ice cream, Frankie who was three and Audrie turning two. The nurse pushed Chrissy to the day room, hauling the oxygen tank beside her. The babies were so happy to see their big sister that they nearly flew into her lap. I can still hear the giggles and then the coughing and then more giggles.

She spent a week in the hospital as she fought off yet another fresh infection. The doctor in charge was a new one. We'd never been to Good Samaritan before. He took me aside and told me that her lungs were severely scarred. The intense coughing had increased the size of her heart and life didn't look good for her. His tone was blunt and matter of fact and I was speechless. As I left the hospital to bundle the children into the car again, I wanted to call Dr. Grach, who would surely set the man straight...

Once home from the hospital, she was the doctor and Audrie was the patient. Since Audrie had rollers in her hair, Chrissy thought she should check her ears because the hair was pulled out of the way. Audrie just let her big sister do whatever she wanted to when they played.

By Christmas time, magic was again in the air. We'd purchased a white canopy bed and chest of drawers for Chrissy and they were propped up against the wall in the basement. The deal was that she could go into the basement if I was downstairs doing laundry or in the sewing room, but she could absolutely never look to her left. She loved the game and walked down the steps with her head turned to the right, then she would

```
TODAY   IS   DECEMBER   18TH  1977

YESTERDAY   I   WENT   TO   A   CHRIST_
MAS   PARTY   FOR   C.F.   (MY DISESE)
CHILDREN   ONLY   AND   WE   TOOK
FRANKIE   AND   AUDRIE   MY   AUNT
ELLEN.   MY   GRANDMA,&   ME   OF
COURSE.   MY   MOM   WENT   EARLY
TO   HELP   WITH   THE   BALLOONS.
   DO   YOU   WANT   ME   TO   TELL
   YOU   WHO   I   SAW:
         SANTA   CLAUS'
         RONALD   MCDONALD
         SMOKEY   THE   BEAR
             A   PLAYER   FROM
         WINTERHAWKS/
LAST   NIGHT   WE   STARTED   GETTING
READY   TO   GET   OUR   CHRISTMAS
TREE   AND   MOVED   THE   FURNITURE
AROUND   SO   WE   COULD   FIND   A
PLACE   TO   PUT   IT.   I   STAYD   UP
   UNTIL   9:30/   WHILE MY   MOM
WENT   SHOPPING   AND   I   STAYD   WI_
TH   MY   DAD.   I   HAD   A   GREAT_
TIME.   I   USEALLY   DO   HAVE   A
GOOD   TIME   WITH   HIM.

             BY:   CHRISTINA   ZACCONE
```

giggle when she found me.

I had been sewing, sewing, sewing and the sewing room had been off limits for weeks. Tonight was Christmas Eve. Traditionally, every December 24, we would join our extended family for Christmas Eve dinner at a local restaurant in Portland and Santa would magically drop by with his bag of presents during our absence. That year, I had created Audrie a stick pony with a large stuffed head filled with lace, frills and cartoons on the fabric. I had braced it against the doorway to my sewing room earlier. I wanted everything in order. Chrissy's bed would, of course, stay downstairs and she could see it when we returned. I planned to rush the horse and Frankie's cowboy boots to the tree while the kids were in the car. But first, I needed to finish Chrissy's Christmas dress for dinner.

In the meantime as my head whirled with what to do next, Chrissy called from upstairs. I'd told her she couldn't surprise me down there as I might be making something for one of her gifts. She loved the intrigue.

"Momma, can I PLEASE come downstairs NOW?"

I'd been thinking of Chrissy as I sewed, wondering if she would soon admit that she doubted Santa's existence. I smiled, wondering when her pretense could be over. I was sure she didn't still believe in the fat, jolly man and I wondered when she would ask me about him. Without thinking through my foggy brain as I put the finishing touches on her red velvet dress, I said, "Sure, but don't look to the left of the stairway…PROMISE?" It was an ongoing game.

She sung, "Okay." I heard her little footsteps and then just as she came around the corner I heard her stop and say in an incredulous voice, "Oh! I didn't know you were making Audrie a little pony."

I froze. My hands stopped and my breath held as I stalled for an answer. That was Audrie's Santa gift. Now what? Chrissy was eight years old. Did she still believe? Did her classmates already tell her there was no Santa? Was she pretending just to keep the magic in the holiday? I turned around in my sewing chair and pushed aside the clothing I was making at the last minute. I saw her looking between me and the pony and her eyebrows rose in confusion.

I opened my arms toward her and she walked slowly into them. I knew she would know if I hedged because she was very quick witted. She hugged me and I assumed it was because she knew the truth, so I launched into a detailed response. "Chrissy, you don't still believe in Santa do you?"

She stiffened in my arms. Oh. My. God. The look on her face was like a hurricane bursting through the clouds. Her eyes teared up, her lips jerked into an "O" and she started sobbing. I can still feel her immense disappointment and her little body shaking as I pulled her onto my lap. I rocked her gently and crooned my love for her. "Oh, honey. I am so sorry. I thought you knew…."

"Noooooooo. You mean it's all pretend?"

"Yes, but it has been fun, huh?" I tried to cover my tracks with humor but it was not working.

After the shudders stopped, she stood up and looked at me. I wiped her eyes and nose and then she backed up and smiled half-heartedly at me. "Momma," she whispered, "PLEASE don't tell grandma that I know until AFTER Christmas, okay?"

I guess I must have laughed a little because she followed up with, "And we can't tell Frankie and Audrie yet because they will be sad. They need to find out by themselves when they get older, okay?"

I smiled at her adult-like response and nodded my assent. "On my honor, sweetheart," I whispered as we walked upstairs hand in hand, sharing our secret and later trying to hide the matter from everyone else.

During that evening at the Red Lion Inn on the Columbia River, there were sixteen of us at our Christmas Eve dinner. As we watched the lighted houseboats float by the restaurant windows blinking and glittering in the Annual Christmas Light Parade, Chrissy glanced my way. Her blue eyes twinkled in that special way I'd grown to love and we shared a conspiratorial smile that nobody understood but us.

She let her laughter escape as she caught my eyes again when her uncles and grandfather pointed their fingers toward the dark sky. Could she see Santa's sleigh flying just out of sight across the river? She better hurry to the window or she would miss the reindeer. Was he on his way to their house to take all the presents? She laughed before charging over to the window to keep the game going for the last time in her little life.

Yes, my girl wanted to pretend one more year. Little did we know that it would be our most precious memory of her last Christmas with us?

I never got over my response to her that Christmas Eve. And when that memory slips across my mind, I'm right back in that sewing room chair and my little girl rounding the corner into the room. Then, her face blanches and she looks as if a bomb went off in her head.

After Chrissy's hospitalization in 1977 where we brought Audrie's birthday party to her, a master plan erupted in Mom and Dad's household.

Disneyland seemed like the perfect place to celebrate her homecoming. First, Mom and Dad wanted to take her there --- just the three of them? What? I had never been there and the thought of my girl enjoying all the firsts that Disneyland offers to children was not going to work for me.

We found sitters for Frankie and Audrie.

We bought airline tickets.

We invited ourselves along.

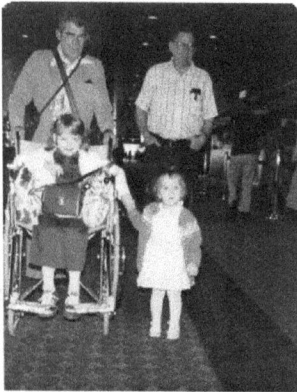 Chrissy was ecstatic (and so was I). Dr. Grach managed to get Chrissy an entrance ticket into Disneyland through the Make a Wish Foundation. Although, she was still weak from the hospitalization and struggled for breath when she coughed, the doctor assured us that it would be a good idea. I read more into her suggestion than just a trip to Disneyland. I looked the other way and ignored the worry etched on her face.

She was delighted to be chauffeured around in a wheel chair all the way to the gate as she held Audrie's hand, wishing her brother and sister could accompany us.

Disneyland made my heart sing as I had never been there before. Watching the awestruck face of my daughter and the constant smiles she gave me in between her coughing spells lingered with me long after I went to bed each night. She tried to trick all of us when she asked for a memento here or there. "You have money, Chrissy, you can buy this yourself."

Those blue eyes looked startled and then she said, "But I'm saving MY money."

I still get choked up when I hear It's a Small World sung over the radio and I am thrown back into the boat with her as we sailed past the dolls singing that song in that Disneyland ride.

Photo: Dad, Chrissy, Mel and Audrie

CHAPTER TWENTY

My girl was admitted to the hospital six weeks later. Chrissy was so full of medications and fearful of being without the oxygen tube to breathe, she was a nervous wreck. When the sun shone through the window of the hospital room, I suggested taking her for a walk in a wheelchair. The thought of going anywhere without the oxygen tank paralyzed her until the nurse put the oxygen tank on a wheeled pole and I pushed it along beside her.

She loved going outside. Trees were abloom. Yellow daffodils, red tulips and lilies of the valley lined the walkways. Spring in Portland is magical after the rain and gloom of winter and flowers peek out of the soil.

We didn't stay outside long.

Medicines filled her days: Pancreatic enzymes, vitamins, sulpha tablets, antibiotics and now diuretics and digitalis to slow down her heart rate. The never-ending cough had indeed enlarged her heart and aged it beyond her years. When the nurse brought the tray of meds, Chrissy shrunk in the bed as if trying to disappear so the nurse couldn't find her.

Now I'm back where I started this memoir.

The most frightening part of the sojourn in the hospital for these weeks, the most painful time of her day is testing and measuring her blood gases. The blood gas test determines how well her lungs are able to move oxygen into the blood and remove carbon dioxide from the blood. Blood must be taken from an artery. For Chrissy, the blood was drawn from the radial artery in her wrist.

To me, it appeared as if the needle was pushed so far into her small wrist, it was as if it went to the bone. The nurse prodded and cranked the needle around in her wrist to draw the substance for the test until Chrissy was crying and I could only hold my breath.

To add to her trauma, some of her medication or the lack of valuable oxygen to her brain caused hallucinations. Everyone was edgy and alarmed. Today was the worst day; just after the respiratory therapist had clapped her, she was exhausted. I snuggled into the chair beside her bed and her favorite nurse Kris stood beside us.

Christina's large blue eyes looked at me every few minutes to make sure I was still there. Ever fearful of being alone, I sat beside her during those last three weeks, like a mainstay in a sinking ship. Now she was finally asleep. The unforgiving coughing spells that had jerked her small body like a volcano, quieted. She had a calm, gentle expression on her face.

Even with my eyes closed, I visualized Chrissy glancing worriedly at the ceiling. Back and forth. Back and forth. Puffy fingers clutched at the flowered sheet covering her frail body and then I saw her eyes change from agitation to terror. Her small arms flailed wildly around the bed, hugging the sheet to her chest, her knuckles white. When she screamed toward the ceiling, I jumped toward her. And then I lay half way across her small body to whisper and sooth her as I tried to understand her hallucinating fears.

"Mommy, Mommy, Mommy...Kris..." Her frightened eyes wouldn't leave the ceiling. Trying to scramble toward her headboard, she pulled herself backwards against the pillow. "Make them go away before they fall on me...the railroad tracks are going to fall on top of me." She was crying and her arms clung to my neck so tightly, I couldn't lift my head. I couldn't breathe.

When I twisted to glance above her bed, I saw the metal strips. They housed the privacy curtain three quarters of the circumference around her bed. Turning back toward her tear-filled face, I smiled. How often did I smile when tears choked my throat? When they welled up dangerously close to the surface and my trembling lips held firm? Every day. And today was one of them while I heard her jagged whispers.

Once her cries subsided, I explained about hallucinations as I pieced her fears together. She was so pumped full of drugs, her mind was playing tricks on her. When I promised the tracks would stay put, she quieted. But she still cried fitfully. I held her in my arms and smoothed my hand over her chest, where her heart beat like a caged bird. I worried it would burst from beneath her Raggedy Ann nightgown.

Once she believed us, she gave a shaky laugh. Kris tickled her feet beneath the covers and waved her pinky finger as she left the room. The small giggle that escaped from Chrissy was music to both our ears. After a long while, her arms loosened from around my neck and she fell asleep. I stretched my arm across the bed to hold her small, puffy hand curled on the flowered sheet.

The black and white checkered corridors are almost silent, no longer trafficked by day noises of food carts, visitors and loud beeps. The aromatic blend of morning food, disinfectant and visitors' flowers has been replaced by the sound of my heartbeat. I must have fallen asleep because it seemed only seconds later, although it was dusk now, that Chrissy woke me with a jolt when she grabbed my hand. The incredulous look on her face brought me up out of the chair and then she gave me a serene smile, unlike anything I had seen these many days past.

"Mommy, I heard Elvis Presley calling me. I saw him. He wanted to hold my hand. He even called my name." Her voice held surprise and not just a little awe.

I tried not to cry. "Sweetheart, it must have been a sweet dream," I whispered and smiled a little.

Chrissy frowned and shook her head adamantly. "NO, it was not a dream. I know it wasn't. Honest, Mom…" Her eyes burned with an intensity that had been missing for a long time. I felt a tingle rush down my spine and felt a chill as I caressed the back of her trembling hand.

She had always shared my love for Elvis from the time she was a child. Chrissy danced around the room with me when I played his music. She knew Blue Suede Shoes by heart and The Wedding Song. She was such a sweet, funny little girl. But Elvis? We both cried from the sadness and the loss when we had learned of his death the previous summer. I patted her hand and pretended I believed her so she would relax again.

Soon afterward, my husband Frank walked into the room. When Chrissy repeated the words about Elvis verbatim, the hair on my head stood up. As he cradled her head to his chest and ran a hand over her soft, blonde hair, he looked at me over her head and fought tears.

She was happy that her Daddy believed her and his presence calmed both of us. Another hallucination she had daily was imagining that he stood outside the room every day. She asked me why Daddy didn't come into the room. Her hallucinations kept butterflies in my belly. He tried to visit as often as he could, but we had two little children home and he couldn't stretch himself to be both places at once. Luckily, my mother-in-law arrived to be with the children to lift the stress from me to stay and for her son, Frank, to go to work.

Chrissy aunts and uncles came to visit as often as they could, but she became clingier as each day passed. My mother visited often and my husband did his best, but Chrissy wilted when I left her unless I stayed until she slept.

She asked me repeatedly to tell her the story about the clowns that I'd written and changed so many times over the years. Each time I told the story, I made up a different version until I felt empty of words. When I couldn't think of a new one, she asked me to tell the one about the little girl who lost her balloon and the little boy who gave his to her. I'd tell her the story quietly as I gently brushed her golden hair across her pillow in long, even strokes. It was fluffy, almost like spun gold. I ran my fingers through its silkiness as she drifted off to sleep. That version was the story I published in 2010 titled, Goodbye Balloon.

As sick as Chrissy felt, her cheerfulness, sense of humor and love for life still amazed us. Her inspiration seemed to enchant the nurses and pride beat strong within me. But those three weeks in the hospital had taken a tremendous toll. My mind raged against the virus that put her in the bed across from me. I was running out of handkerchiefs from the tears. Many times during those days my Mom or my husband would give me a break. I would race home, shower, change clothes and return to her bedside. Often, on the trip back to the hospital, I prayed that my two young children would one day understand that hellish time in our lives and why I was gone every day. I loved them madly, but I am sure they didn't feel it in those days.

Unfortunately, they only remembered the night I tore out of the house with Chrissy while she fought for breath from a terrible cold. The children had colds of their own, so they were not allowed to visit their sister in the hospital. It seemed like six months instead of twenty some days. The doctors did not want to risk further infection, but as I look back on that time, it grieves me that I gave into their worries. What difference could it have made?

Frank and Audrie both wondered where their big sister was when I came home at the end of the day. I remember how difficult it was to leave Chrissy and then again, how I ached because my two little ones saw so little of me. Oftentimes, they were already in bed when I arrived home and it plagues me still.

Chrissy was very disappointed that she couldn't see Frank who was three and a half and little Audrie, two, because she adored them. I can still hear the laughter in the air as I remember how their antics charmed her. If I could have bottled that up, I'd take it out and listen to the tinkle of their voices.

She was just making progress with Audrie by teaching her to say Chrissy. Audrie listened, stared at her big sister's mouth as she repeated her name and then said, "EH-eeeee." To Audrie, she was saying *Chrissy*. Chrissy was delighted with her baby sister's garbled attempts.

Each day, they asked me the same question, "Where's Chrissy?" Their little voices rang in my ears when I was away from them. And I constantly practiced not crying.

Now, as evening passed into late night, time slipped by me in small, careful movements. Her hard coughing spasms diminished. I watched her sleep and held her fingers curled in the palm of my hand. I was relieved. But my chest crimped with tightness again as I remembered the doctors' words from the morning before. They'd been in and out of her room the past few days and their faces didn't invite hope. Because there was no hope as far as they were concerned.

The night dragged toward dawn. I still pretended she would be all right again. Earlier, tired of crying, I left her room and went home to my two little children and my husband. I used the shower as my haven and let water spill over me, because I could sob aloud where nobody heard me.

No matter how hard I tried, my mind chatter forced the memory of Dr. Grach's words into my head. I tried to silence her voice from earlier that morning, but they pounded at me.

"Chrissy won't be leaving the hospital this time…" It felt like the air had been punched out of my lungs and my spark of hope diminished.

The doctor, who was also my friend by then, had lifted her wet, dark eyes to my face. As they met mine, we stood locked in a gaze that dropped all pretensions. We were both miserable and heart sore and neither of us tried to hide it. She opened her arms wide, inviting me into her embrace as she pressed her firm cheek against my tear-stained face. We hugged hard for a brief time before we stood back.

"You must not show Chrissy your pain, Patricia. I know it will be one of the hardest things you will have to do, but you know how important it is. Dry your tears and remember Chrissy is looking to you for her comfort and love." Dr. Grach caressed my back as we walked down the hallway to Chrissy's room. Her eyes had filled up again before nodding and then she'd walked away.

Chrissy had given me a clear opportunity to share the truth with her. But I was afraid because the enormity of that burden made me shy away from it. The day had left me emotionally drained, flushed and frightened. I squeezed my eyes shut to stop the tears from slipping out of my eyes and down my face as I recalled the conversation.

"Mommy, am I going to die?" She'd asked me the question earlier that evening, full of the question, but not full of the fear I expected. Fear that consumed me.

"No, sweetheart...well, yes, we all die some day and go to heaven," I lied to Chrissy, holding her hand and stroking it, noticing the swelling and loving her so dearly. I traced my fingers over the puffy skin and held it firmly. And for this I felt a measure of guilt. I allowed the burden to overwhelm me, but somehow I kept the ready tears from spilling over.

"But, Mommy, are you sure...I mean are you sure I'm not going to die *now*? Her eyes implored me for an answer she seemed to already know.

I reached over and kissed her forehead soothingly and raised her hand to my cheek. "No, you'll be better tomorrow, sweetheart," I lied again. "Why are you asking me, because you are afraid of what the doctors and nurses do to you when they try to help you feel better?" My voice crumpled but I fought the trembling to prove my statement was not a lie.

"No...not that." She watched me steadily and whispered, "I love you, Mommy." Then she smiled a strange little smile and quietly closed those lovely blue eyes and squeezed my hand good night, gripping me tightly. "Stay close," she murmured.

I had no intention of leaving.

That evening darkness rushed in and quiet surrounded me. My mother tiptoed into the room. When she placed a small bag on the linoleum floor beside the remaining lounge chair, she whispered, "I hope you don't mind my coming back this evening, honey. I was sitting at home when I suddenly felt the need to spend the night with you and Chrissy. You don't mind, do you?"

"Of course not, you're always welcome," I said with a tired smile and reached up to accept her hug and quick kiss. She tiptoed towards Chrissy's bed and touched her hand as she lay asleep, kissed her forehead and smoothed her bangs; then returned to the chair to prepare her bed.

Just before dawn, Chrissy was sleeping soundly without the fluid-sounding wheezing that normally filled the room. It startled me awake because it was unusual to see her relaxing, even in slumber. Darkness was all around us except for the small nightlight. My legs were cramped from sleeping in the chair, my arm asleep from holding her hand in my all-night vigil.

Seeing her asleep, one would never guess that Cystic Fibrosis ravaged her small body. Her skin is normally fair and pink, not pale like many other CF children. The golden strands of her hair still spilled across her white pillow. She hadn't moved her head since I brushed it hours ago. Still, no coughing. "Thank you, Lord," I whispered.

The Cystic Fibrosis induced illness slowed her down physically, but her indomitable spirit refused to be crushed. The bacteria had invaded her weak lungs numerous times in the past, but its presence never lessened her enthusiasm for life or my capacity to die a little each time she was sick.

I glanced over at my mother, who was sleeping fitfully. Her strength constantly amazed me. I am strong for her and she is strong for me. This is ironic since we are both in our own little worlds of fear, pain and love for this child.

I recalled my daughter's tired voice again, just before she fell asleep tonight and that special way she had of saying, "I love you, Mommy."

I got up to hug her once again and even though I knew I might wake her, I caressed her hand and arm slowly in a rhythmic motion as it lay across the coverlet. I noticed again how her hair seemed like a bright halo feathered around her face.   My chest and throat filled up with pressure. I could not move.

I had a sudden flash of memory like a movie as I sat down again, remembering when I was first so intoxicated with her.   So long ago. Nearly nine years. My mind flew back to that day, another place, another time. It seemed a hundred years ago. It was that time in every woman's life that always stays so clearly embedded in her mind.   A flood of memories washed over me like a tidal wave as I watched my mother and daughter sleep.

Chrissy's breathing slowed and her lashes fluttered as she slept. Her fluffed hair splashed across the pillow like rays of sunshine. I stroked the strands as her breathing turned shallow. My heart beat faster.

The nurse's chatter increased and the halls became more active to belie my aloneness. And yet I had never felt so alone in my life. My eyes wandered for the hundredth time to the solitary bed in the corner of the room. The sun began to stream through the east windows of the hospital room. It should have given me solace that she would see another glorious sunrise from her bed. The red Amaryllis, growing by leaps and bounds, stood against the awe-inspiring background of Mt. Hood.   Its showy leaves spurted upward, but a sad loneliness filled my throat and tears crushed my aching heart.

When Chrissy's breathing turned raspy, the sound brought my head around. Maybe the medication was finally going to surprise all of us and we could prove the doctors wrong? My eyes flew toward her. My arm was asleep as it lay across the bed, still wrapped around her small hand. Pin pricks stabbed me from my shoulder to the tips of my fingers. She squeezed my hand tightly for an instant and I knew her fight was over. The mind chatter had won. Everything was still and I couldn't move. My little girl fought valiantly, but she was gone.

The litany suddenly changed inside my head as small lights burst forth. I felt bereft, alone, even though Mom was beside me.

FAIRYDUST TO DAFFODILS   Patricia Steele

"Chrissy…honey….Chrissy….Nurse!" I yelled into the corridor. The nurses came at my call. Intense guilt engulfed me. She'd asked for honest answers but my fear of losing her to the dreaded disease that finally claimed her, weighed heavily. The clamor of people surrounded us in the room, but the sounds faded and I unplugged from reality.

The dreams died. The hopes died. All thoughts died. Numbness devoured my body and soul as I remained still and silently rubbed her soft pale cheek. And I could not let go of her little hand.

CHAPTER TWENTY ONE

Overwhelming grief shook my heart, but then I felt numbness creep over me; its distinct feeling of love and peace left me breathless. In its stead, was the glow of Chrissy's legacy. She tried to tell me, urged me to face her dying. She wanted me to talk about it. Embrace it. But I couldn't do it. And then I imagined the flutter of angel's wings, her gift to me.

Losing my daughter that morning placed me in a special realm of understanding as I forged through life all the years after. I raised my beautiful toddlers, who are now adults. I also ended my twenty-two year marriage sixteen years afterward when my heart told me to do so.

Chrissy's reach for honesty made me realize the gift she opened in my heart. Just like the spiritual painting with Jesus at the door without a handle because He must be invited in…I didn't realize what she was asking me until she had walked through it onto the other side.

Today, I have forgiven myself for lying to Chrissy that night. I wanted to be gentle with her soul. Fantasy tells me she watches over me and her brother and sister. I realize, now, I lied to myself and she was watching me all the time. I believe, where we are --- peace must be and Chrissy knew it before I did.

No one can ever fully erase the pain of losing a child. Now, years later, that early morning feels like a dream. The intense grief has faded, although sad melancholy lingers. Sometimes I am startled to find myself in Chrissy's hospital room and it is again 1978.

I found a new meaning for the word eternity. I read somewhere that eternity can be measured by picking up one grain of sand and placing it on the opposite shore of the ocean. Afterward, you take another grain of sand from that shore and bring it back to the original shore. And then you repeat the trip, travel and return until each grain of sand on our shore is transferred to the other. That's eternity. Never again would I…never again would she…never again.

Daffodils still burst forth each spring. When their bright heads appear above the soil, rejoicing in the sunshine, I give a feeble smile at the yellow beauties. And each year on March 15, I wake up thinking of Chrissy and that day so long ago when the fairydust sprinkled around me. This year in 2018, she would have turned forty nine years old.

My memories are forever etched on my heart. Her death shook me to my core. Both my emotions and conscience were raw for a very long time and I did not know how to get past the pain.

Joe Biden put it succinctly when he talked about the constant weight of grief in 2012 after his son died from cancer. "Just when you think, maybe I'm going to make it, you are riding down the road and you pass a field, and you see a flower and it reminds you. Or you hear a tune on the radio. Or you just look up into the night. You think, maybe I'm not going to make it, man. Because there will come a day --- I promise you, and your parents as well --- when the thought of your son or daughter, or your husband or wife, brings a smile to your lips before it brings a tear to your eye. It will happen."

The man was right. After Chrissy died from congestive heart failure, my mind played tricks on me. When I saw a small girl with blonde hair skipping down the street, standing in line at the grocery store or laughing with her head thrown back, I would hear white noise in my head. Or when I dreamed one night that the phone rang years after she died and a little girl's voice said, "Mommy, why aren't you coming to visit me? Nobody is coming to see me." Nightmares like that rarely ravage my sleep anymore and for that I am thankful, but it was a long difficult journey to get here.

During my grieving process, someone suggested that I write a letter to Chrissy. After many starts and stops, I have finally put a gentle closure on my grief by writing this memoir and the following letter helped put me there.

Christina Marie Zaccone

BIRTH	15 Mar 1969
	Salem, Marion County, Oregon, USA
DEATH	25 Feb 1978 (aged 8)
	Portland, Multnomah County, Oregon, USA
BURIAL	Willamette National Cemetery
	Portland, Multnomah County, Oregon, USA
PLOT	N, 0, 2248
MEMORIAL ID	1357694 · View Source

Photo added by Nathan Haines

Dear Chrissy,

That blurry day so long ago has been brought to your mother's mind once again for the hundredth time. This time, though, it's different. That day we were both very frightened. Our hearts both beat fiercely, each for fear of losing the other, me to life and you to death. And yet, I know instantly upon the recreation of that day in 1978 when you held my hand for that last time, that we were gently but ultimately saying goodbye. Your life was more precious to me than a child could ever know. I am telling you now --- I am feeling a loss, but more strength too.

You were really the strong one. We each knew what was happening. You came to grips with the reality and met it head on. You admitted your fears to me, but I avoided the reality and hid mine from you. We missed some very special conversations because of my inability to allow myself to believe you were dying.

Please forgive me. Your life and death were more moving to me than anything that has come before or after. Your life, though...Ah – that was my gift. You left me with some insights that only I have just recently allowed myself to understand.

I was angry that you could face death and I could not. I was angry at your charm and docility when I felt only disbelief and helplessness. I was angry that I could not change the course of the disease to save you. And I was so very proud of you, my darling, because you accepted it.

I will miss you always.

All my love and heart songs,

Momma

Fairydust still tumbles around me as I remember the loveliness she added to my life. Remembering that little girl, her impish personality, her brand of special girlhood, all of that…and the fairydust is still there. I can no longer feel it swirling around the room or bumping against me, but I know it is there.

So each springtime, when the daffodils are in bloom, I am reminded that inside each flower head, fairydust exists. Maybe not as sparkly as it was in 1969, but whispering through my heart nevertheless.

I have spent the better part of the morning thinking about Chrissy. She would be nearly fifty years old today, five years older than my son Frank and six years older than my daughter Audrie.

On March 15, 1997 Chrissy would have turned twenty eight years old. On that day, my son Frank and his wife were in the delivery room at Kaiser Permanente in Portland, Oregon. It will always be a mystical day for our family because my granddaughter, Frankie Christina Zaccone was born. Frank told me when he realized it was his big sister's birthday when his daughter came into the world, he couldn't hold back his tears.

Today, Christina would be auntie to four nieces (Frankie Christina, Kadence, Hillary and Colby and two nephews, Dylan and Grant. She would also be a great aunt to a little boy named Travis.

Christina

Wherever we are and whatever we do,
Surround us always are visions of you
The sunny sheen of your soft, blonde hair,
The blue of your eyes, the love light there,
The warmth of your arms, your voice so dear,
All these fond memories keep you near.
We made you smile and watched you grow
And oh, my darling, we miss you so,
And wherever we are and whatever we do,
There's no one at all takes the place of you.

Based on the poem by E. Myrtle Terry (my grandmother) to her husband, Earl.

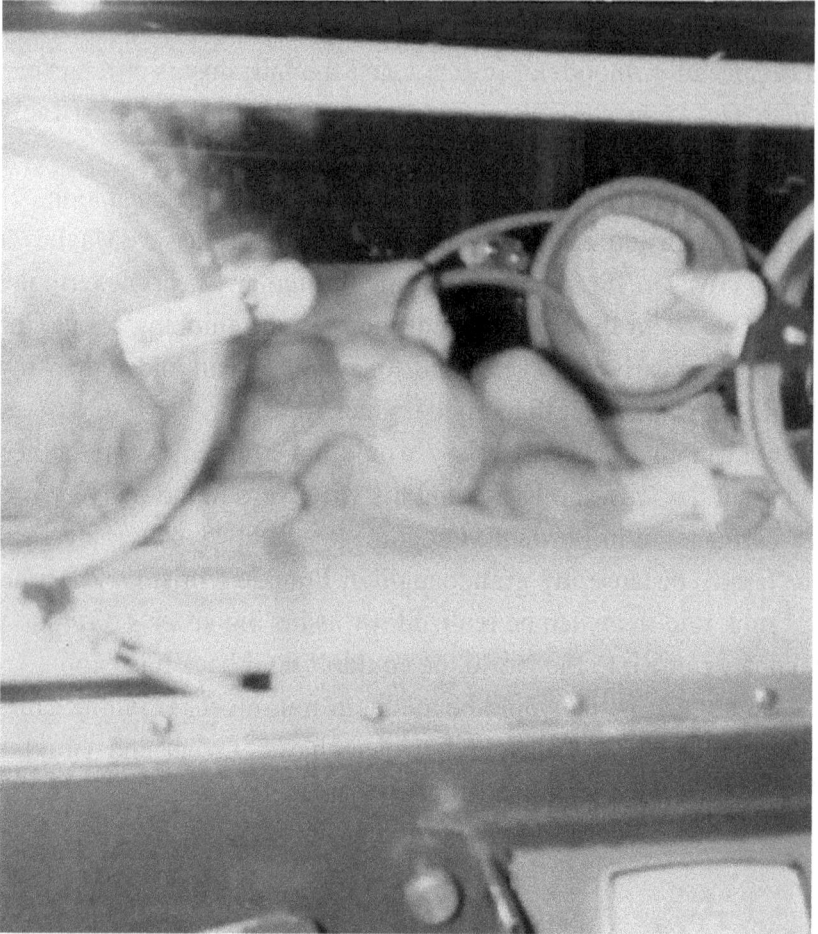

Christina Marie
March 17, 1969
Doernbecker Hospital, OHSU
Portland, Oregon

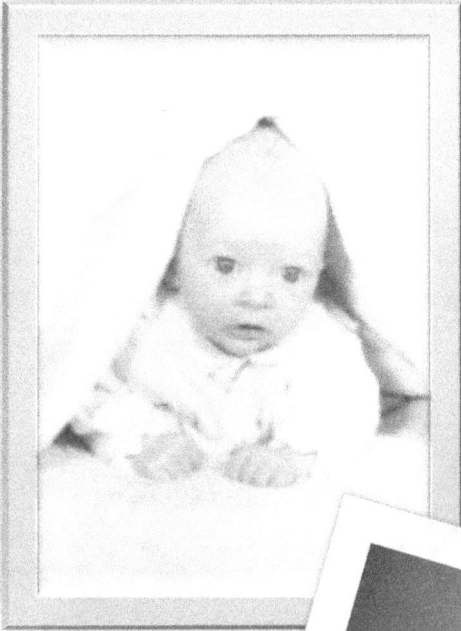

Christina
June, 1969
Portland, Oregon

Below: September, 1969
Portland, Oregon
This photo was taken at
our small apartment on
SE 15th Avenue during
my first separation when
she was a little wildfire
racing around in her
walker.

She was getting used to the photographer by now and gave up the fight because she had a camera pointing at her so often.

    Christina Marie

    9 months old

    Portland, Oregon

She loved looking at pictures of her family. One of her favorites was a four-generation photo of her with me, grandma and great-grandma Myrtle Terry. She would cozy up to it and stare at it sometimes and I always wondered about the little conversation that flowed through her mind

The summer after her second year, we took a road trip to California. My Spanish grandmother, whom I called abuelita, was the queen of flower gardens. When she saw Chrissy for the first time, she kept wiping her eyes to stop the tears. Abuelita loved showing her the flowers and Chrissy put her nose in every blossom. I can still hear her saying, "Mmmmmmmmm." Abuelita laughed at her response and I am sure that little girl must have smelled a hundred blooms that day in Vacaville

The Lions Club typically donates glasses in their organization. However, Chrissy's recent surgery repaired her eye muscle and she did not need glasses anymore. The Lions Club decided to make an exception that year because Chrissy's CF needs were important to the group. Instead, they donated the funds to buy her nebulizer and mist tent. No more need to rent the equipment because suddenly we owned it. The local newspaper printed the story and this photo.

Christmas 1973
Girard, Ohio

Spring 1975, Girard, Ohio

The day this photo was taken, we were visiting a friend with two teenage daughters. Chrissy followed the girls upstairs to their bedroom to listen to records. While I was downstairs, I heard footsteps pattering down the stairs and she was laughing.

"Momma, I heard a song from the olden days and it was so funny."

"Really? What was it?"

"Ba ba ba ba Barbara Ann
 Ba ba ba ba Barbara Ann
 Ba ba ba ba Barbara Ann (take my hand)
 Ba ba ba ba Barbara Ann
 Ba ba ba ba Barbara Ann
 You've got me rockin' and a-rollin' Rockin' and a-reelin'
 Barbara Ann
 Ba ba ba ba Barbara AnnBa-ba-ba…ba Barbara ann."

(Ha Ha - I sang the song in my high school days.)

1974 – Chrissy was five years old. Her Aunt Sheryl made her a cape and she felt like a princess. When the package arrived from Oregon, she wanted to wear it every day. She primped around the house and swirled around on her toes like a ballerina. I see I was already drinking wine…or maybe I'd just finished it (?)

Chrissy was four years old when grandpa and grandma Bettencourt arrived to visit us in July 1974. When she watched her swing set being put together, she hopped on both feet and ran around the swing, impatient to get on it.

She spent hours of playtime on the swing set before we left Ohio and moved to Oregon in July 1975.

Robbie Mook was her favorite playmate, a neighbor boy whose aunt was my sister-in-law, Judy Zaccone. She and Robbie's mother were twin sisters and I could not remember a day when he wasn't knocking on our door.

Summer 1976, Girard, Ohio

Living next door to grandma and grandpa was magical for Chrissy. She often lugged her baby brother around and sometimes their playtime was downstairs around their grandpa's pool table. Dad was always patient as long as the children followed the rules...no cue stick pointed to the green felt. No throwing pool balls. Chrissy and her Uncle Carl played pool and she learned more rules. And then she wanted to teach her brother Frankie. This photo still hangs on my parent's downstairs wall even though the pool table is long gone.

Christmas time for children is always magical in our family. Chrissy wanted Frankie and Audrie to love the holiday like she did and sang Christmas songs and pointed out Santa Claus to them in her books. She helped the babies unwrap their gifts and kept them from removing the Christmas ornaments. Once, she caught one just as a glass bulb left Frankie's hand to throw it across the room.

Linda and I tried to find time for the little cousins to spend time together either by my going to Albany or Linda brought Michele to Portland. They were often shy of one another because each time they met after time in between, it was like a new conversation.

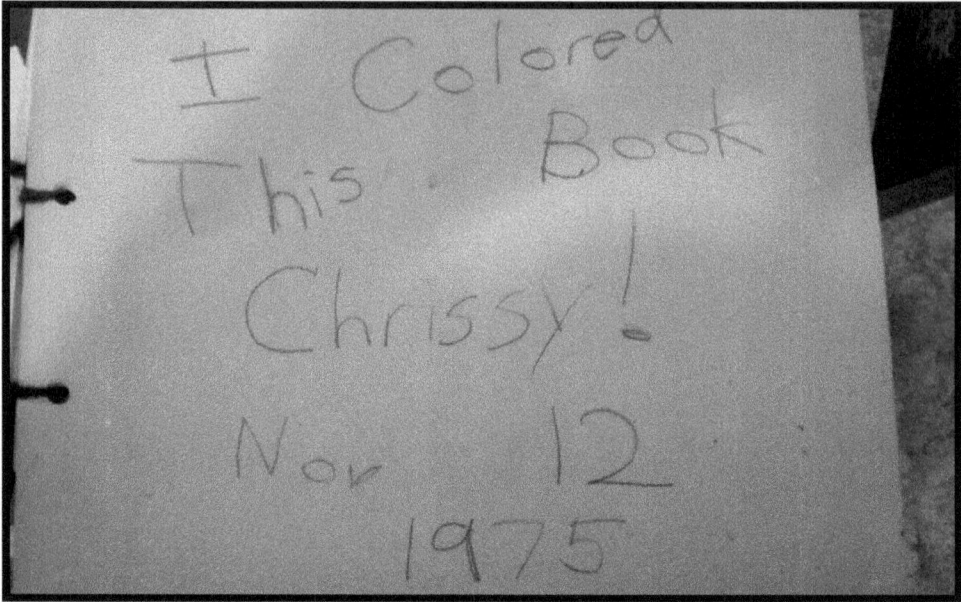

Chrissy liked to draw pictures, color them and then create books. She couldn't quite figure out the hole punch, so she would run to me to get it started. Then, she would get a ball of yarn and thread it through all the pages. I guess we had our own publishing company in the house.

From: Your friend Chrissy zaccone

1976

To: Santa Claus
North Pole
U.S.A.

Dear Santa Claus   12-6-76 Night
I have always wanted a calculator
of my very own, and this year I wish
you would Please bring me one.
Could you please bring my brother
a "Big Wheel"
Maybe you could bring Audrie a
Jumping Horse. She'd like that.
I sure did like it when you
called me last year.
Last year I heard bells in the sky
and I saw a red light, too.
                              zaccone
My Grandma that wants a
candy cane, please.
I tried so much to be good all
year thru.   Love, Chrissy
                              zaccone

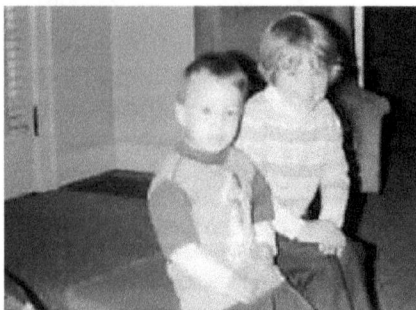

Frankie wanted to go with Chrissy when she went to summer camp. She sat on the suitcase to keep stop him from unlatching it and pulling everything out again. This photo was taken when she got wise and just sat on it. He thought it was a game and joined her.

Grandma and Grandpa took Chrissy on a camping trip to the Oregon beach in 1977 where she had their undivided attention. She learned to cook marshmallows and make s'mores. She loved laying in the top of their camper and looking out the little window toward the beach.

The beauty of living next door to my parents in Portland was that my children often ran back and forth between us. My Mom told the story of Chrissy coming over to ask what she was fixing for dinner at her house. She wanted to eat the meal grandma made if she liked it better than mine.

Another time when Mom was washing off her dining room table, Chrissy said, "Why don't you clean off the table like Mommy does?"
"Well, how does your Mommy do it?"
Chrissy put her hand on the table and then swiped the crumbs onto the floor.
What? My Mom laughed and I just shook my head.

And then there was the day she listened to my Mom's old 78 record and she heard my childish voice recite, Hey, diddle, diddle. She came home to tell me she heard a record that was "about ninety years old."
Hey, diddle, diddle,
The cat and the fiddle,
The cow jumped over the moon;
The little dog laughed
To see such sport,
And the dish ran away with the spoon

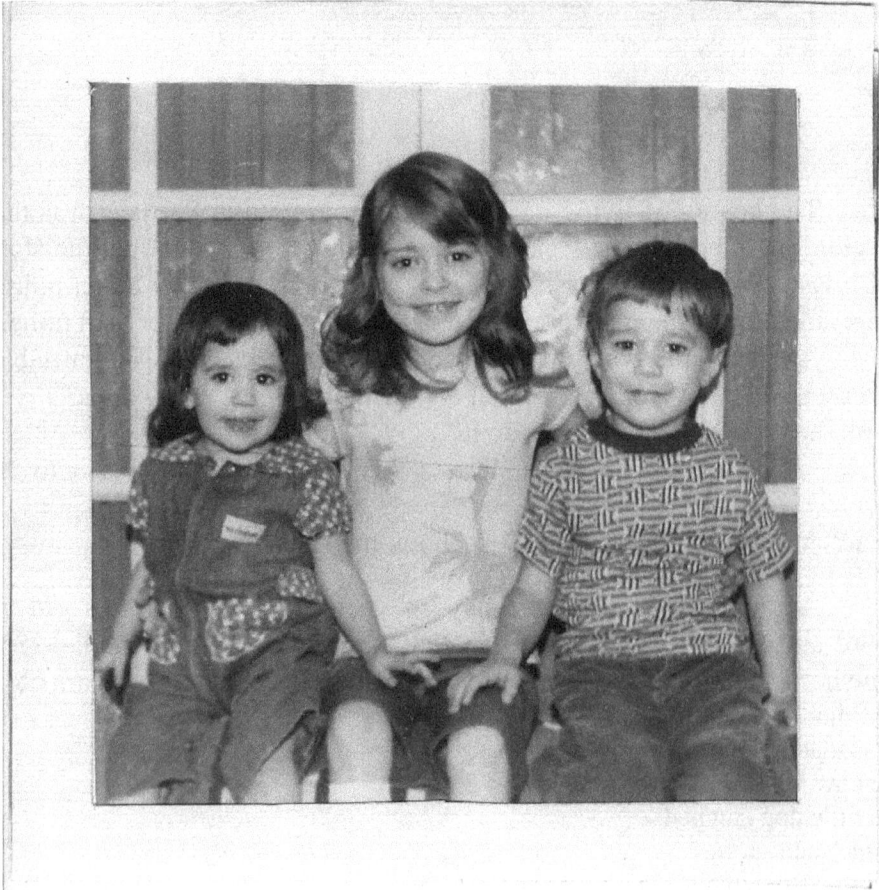

CLINICAL DEFINITIONS

Optimal management of cystic fibrosis (CF) is complex and time-consuming. The daily regimen for CF typically begins in the morning and ends at bedtime and may require an investment of over an hour a day on the part of both parent and child. Components of the treatment regimen often include taking oral and nebulized medications, doing chest physiotherapy, engaging in regular exercise, and eating and drinking to reach increased fat and calorie recommendations.

It may also include taking supplemental enzymes, insulin, receiving parenteral nutrition, and completing sinus care. Chest physiotherapy, or airway clearance treatments, aka ACTs, are typically prescribed twice daily for 15-30 minutes each, depending on the method used, and may be increased to four times daily if the child shows signs of acute illness. These treatments loosen mucus[3] from the lungs, and with the aid of special "huff coughs," move it to the upper airways from which it can be expelled. Failure to do airway clearance contributes to plugged airways with loss of pulmonary function. Depending on the child's age, motor skills and preferences, the treatment may be accomplished through chest percussions (in which parents physically clap the child's back and sides in a particular pattern), or by wearing a vest that mechanically vibrates the child, or handheld devices which send vibrations into the lungs when a child breathes into them. Regardless of the method, parental presence is usually required for children, whether to actually perform the treatment on the child's body, to prepare the equipment and clean it, or to supervise older children completing these tasks independently.

J Clin Psychol Med Settings. Author manuscript; available in PMC 2015 Jun 1.
Published in final edited form as:
J Clin Psychol Med Settings. 2014 Jun; 21(2): 125–135.
doi: 10.1007/s10880-014-9396-1

---

[3] Mucus is a noun and mucus is an adjective. So, the actual fluid that comes out of your nose when you are congested is mucus and the linings in your body that secrete mucus are mucus membranes. ... The word actually derives straight from the Latin word mucus, meaning 'snot, slime, or mold.

COUGHING: Although coughing can help move mucus out of the larger airways, it is not effective for moving mucus out of the smaller ones. This is why coughing should be done with other airway clearing techniques, which are more effective at moving mucus up from the smaller airways into the larger ones, where it can be coughed out.

With CF, you shouldn't try to suppress coughs, or keep yourself from coughing. To avoid spreading germs, you can cough into a tissue, throw it away and then clean your hands with an alcohol-based hand gel.

HUFFING: Huffing, (huff coughing) is a technique that helps move mucus from the lungs. It is typically done in combination with another ACT such as postural drainage. It involves taking a breath in, holding it and actively exhaling. This technique enables air to get behind the mucus and separates it from the lung wall so it can be blown out. Huffing is not as forceful as a cough, but it is less tiring. Huffing is like exhaling onto a mirror to steam it up.

The Huff Coughing Technique:
Sit up straight with chin tilted slightly up and mouth open. Take a slow deep breath to fill lungs about three quarters full. Hold breath for two or three seconds. Exhale forcefully, but slowly, in a continuous exhalation to move mucus from the smaller to the larger airways. Repeat this maneuver two more times and then follow with one strong cough to clear mucus from the larger airways. Do a cycle of four to five huff coughs as part of your airway clearance.

POSTURAL DRAINAGE:
With postural drainage, the person lies or sits in various positions so the part of the lung to be drained is as high as possible. That part of the lung is then drained using percussion, vibration and gravity. When the person with CF is in one of the positions, the caregiver can clap on the person's chest wall. This is usually done for three to five minutes and is sometimes followed by vibration over the same area for approximately 15 seconds (or during five exhalations). The person is then encouraged to cough or huff forcefully to get the mucus out of the lungs.

Clapping (percussion) by the caregiver on the chest wall over the part of the lung to be drained helps move the mucus into the larger airways. The hand is cupped as if to hold water but with the palm facing down (as shown in the figure below). The cupped hand curves to the chest wall and traps a cushion of air to soften the clapping.

www.ingramcontent.com/pod-product-compliance
Lightning Source LLC
Chambersburg PA
CBHW061821040426
42447CB00012B/2750